GEORGE BURTON

George Burton at the Mayflower, 1965

GEORGE BURTON

A Study in Contradictions

by

DAVID and JEAN HEWITT

HODDER AND STOUGHTON

Printed in Great Britain for Hodder and Stoughton Limited, St. Paul's House, Warwick Lane, London, E.C.4 by Ebenezer Baylis and Son, Limited, The Trinity Press, Worcester, and London.

To
The Christian Church
of the
Mayflower Family Centre

Authors' Preface

George Burton wanted his life story to be written and left to us all his films, papers and letters for this purpose. In addition we have had access to the Mayflower Family Centre's library of tape recordings, so that quotes from his speeches are verbatim.

We are indebted to many sources, oral and written, in particular to the late Lt.-Col. Percy Coriat's *Soldier in Oman*. The short quotation on page 32 is taken from *Bugles and a Tiger* by John Masters (Michael Joseph). We are grateful to William Heinemann Ltd. for permission to quote from Allan Bullock's *The Life and Times of Ernest Bevin*. We would like to acknowledge help given by many people through personal interviews and correspondence.

Special mention is due to others who helped us in various ways: Mrs. Helena Burton, Rev. David S. Sheppard, Miss Rosemary Finch, Miss Joan de Torre; the Mayflower Family Centre members; Matthew Dieppe and Rev. Ian D. Elliott; Rev. John C. Pollock; Mrs. Jean Bullen and Mrs. Edith Smith; Mrs. Elsie Affolter for her tireless typing; the Vicar and people of St. Simon and St. Jude's Church for tolerating a part-time curate.

David and Jean Hewitt

Southport
January 1969

Contents

Illustrations

Foreword

Everything about George Burton was ten feet tall. His adventures, his disasters, his good points and his bad ones, all seemed larger than life. He had great personal magnetism, and those of us who worked closely with him sometimes asked ourselves if we were not just under his spell when we thought of him as a great man. I can only say that, writing over two years after his death, he has no rival in my mind for "the most unforgettable character I ever met". He had a brilliant brain, racing ahead of all of us; when eventually he found himself accepted and appreciated, he influenced people deeply, lastingly and far beyond Canning Town.

If ever there was a mixed-up kid it was George. Yet if ever there was a life in which I saw God doing great things through a human being, it was his. This book makes us all look honestly at ourselves. The most significant lesson I learn from it is that such an earthy man can be a powerful instrument for God. Many Christians give up in despair; "I'm too bad, I'm no use"; "I've not got the right background or the right training". What we read about in this book is the faith and the courage truly to believe in Christ's forgiveness and His promise to give strength in areas of our life and at moments when we feel at our weakest. Here is no easy conversion story; rather it is the story of the failure of a Christian life. At thirty-six he was a piece of human wreckage. Then came the painful rehabilitation and after that the striking way God used the experience so painfully gathered, his strengths often closest to his weaknesses.

David and Jean Hewitt have not over-written the story. If their purpose had been to portray the most colourful picture possible, there was much they could have added. They have reproduced faithfully the extraordinary contradictions there were in George Burton; the gaiety and the bitter unhappiness; the understanding love and the streak of cruelty; far-seeing vision and crippling introspection. The contradictions were all true and David and Jean saw them as closely as anyone. This book was born both from first hand experience and from thorough research.

Our consciences have to face questions about the society which created, or tolerated, the conditions in which George grew up. On the surface everything is different now. Indeed it is a great mistake to think in terms of slums and poverty. Yet George found much in common between Canning Town in the 1960s and the Glasgow he had known in the 1920s. In the great industrial areas of big cities most young people, unless they have a particular sort of academic intelligence, are blocked from developing as they could. Many have received enough education to refuse to sit down tamely under boredom, but not enough to know how to use their increased leisure and money. If we believe that "The earth is the Lord's and the fullness thereof" we should see that we have a great responsibility to work for a society in which fulfilment at work and in leisure is far more possible. George was limited in his recognition of this need, but he had great understanding of those who have grown up in such areas.

George Burton challenged the assumptions of many of us. By what right did we assume that middle-class values were necessarily Christian values? Why should we assume that people from a non-reading background could not become thoughtful, deeply-committed Christians? Why should we not expect leaders to emerge from our community in Canning Town as much as anywhere else? This story includes some great disappointments among young people he tried to help; I believe that some of these will one day come back to deep Christian commitment as George himself did. But it also includes some who are continuing with great ability the work that he began.

This book brings a challenge to the whole Christian Church and to the Youth Service too. There is a place, as he eventually acknowledged, for highly trained leadership. Yet this untrained, uncouth, disturbing, tangled-up man, who really believed in the power of God, taught us all. We have to ask if we expect God to produce others of the same order, and whether we will make room for them.

David S. Sheppard

Mayflower Family Centre
London, E.16
January 1969

Prologue

"What's the matter, Sue?" A fleshy figure in slippers, open-necked shirt, and crumpled trousers loosened at the waist, sprawled back in his arm chair. An electric fire scorched up at him from the paper-strewn floor. A small table supporting a tray of dirty crockery stood between him and the blonde teenager he was addressing. Sue sat awkwardly on the divan in her youth leader's flat. Her silence, followed by a sob, gave him the answer to his question. "Do your parents know?" "Cor blimey, no! They'd chuck me out," she wailed. She had come to the one person she could trust with her secret.

There was a knock at the door. "The party of clergymen has arrived," John announced. "Show them up into the other room," George ordered. "You can stay around, John, and see how I handle this lot." Then George sauntered in, hands in pockets. One of the group sprang to his feet and introduced himself as a diocesan youth chaplain. "I'm not interested in who you are or what qualifications you've got," George told him. "Have you ever led a soul to the Lord?" Then he went on, "I suppose you've all come to shake hands with the Reverend David Sheppard. Well, *I'm* in charge of the youth work here." Picking up a *New English Bible* from a chair he tossed it across the room, gloating over their looks of horror. "One of my young people came to Christ after reading a Bible which she picked off the floor," he declared by way of justification. Sensing the visitors were not convinced, he marched them on a hasty tour of the Mayflower Family Centre, ostentatiously interviewing whoever he met about their conversion experience. Many of the clergymen had the impression that he was in desperate need of mental treatment.

George retired to the kitchen and planted himself at the table. "Make me a nice pot of tea, Dilys, and some eggy bacon," he briefed the housekeeper, "and I want some of that crusty bread." Dutifully Dilys set the frying-pan sizzling. "How's that attractive daughter of yours?" he inquired of the daily help. "Is she still courting?" Before he could hear the reply, there was a phone call from Gran whose crises over non-payment of her rent were familiar to George. This time she was being threatened with eviction. "Look, Gran," he told her. "I can't come tonight, but tomorrow it's my day off, so I'll be up to see you first thing in the morning."

Spirits were unusually high in the youth club that evening and George kept on the move from the main club room to the open-air playground, then to the boxing gym and the free for all 'beating-up room'. His progress was punctuated by a score of pointed conversations with boys and girls about their jobs, their court cases, their fashions, and their romances. At ten his voice resounded through the buildings, "Good night, everyone," and the teenagers drifted out. A billiard ball sped towards him and he leapt deftly to avoid a crack on the ankle. "Get out!" he blazed and the club room emptied, except for his band of helpers. "How many of you spoke to anyone about Christ this evening?" he challenged them. No one stirred. "Nor did I," he admitted. "But that's what we're here for. It may take months before they'll accept you, but keep praying and expecting God to use you." The little group bowed in prayer before dispersing, some to the other end of London.

"Come on, Michael," he turned to the young man beside him. "You can enlarge your education tonight. I've got to visit a couple of homes and you can come with me." They drove out into the streets of Canning Town and headed towards the docks. Seated in Mollie's home George explained, "I've had you on my mind all day, and I couldn't go to bed without seeing how you were." She had recently been discharged from hospital and was frightened about her illness. Fred, her husband, was busy painting the door of the adjoining room. George offered Michael's services and the job was soon finished. "Let's thank God for the way He has brought you through these months," George suggested as they rose to go.

It was midnight before George climbed wearily to his flat, for on the way back he had called on a couple whose marriage was undergoing strains. His visit coincided with a heated row, but the tension was broken by his timely counsel and he left the couple relaxed and smiling.

Who was this man, so rudely aggressive to some, yet so tenderly sensitive to others? The extraordinary character who hit the Mayflower Family Centre in 1958 had a strange background which was unfolded to his colleagues in the following years.

His childhood poverty scarred George Burton with a sense of inferiority which his natural ambition drove him to conquer. He succeeded, at the cost of considerable mental strain, for his pose of brash authority veiled tormenting anxieties. To combat his fears of failure and ridicule he manipulated people mercilessly.

Yet even George's weaknesses were harnessed by God to the single task of training Christian leaders in the unlikely environment of Canning Town. His common touch helped him to identify himself with the people, and he believed unshakably that they were capable of taking responsibility. This conviction was partly inspired by his hatred of middle-class snobbery.

To function properly George Burton needed a team within which to vent his egotism and desire to dominate. He inspired them, but they for their part often had to carry him through times of personal stress. The Mayflower's Warden, David Sheppard, had already learnt, as the Rev. Maurice Wood observed, to subordinate "his natural gifts of leadership so that he was a captain working with a team rather than a leader working over a team".

A number of 'ifs' hang over George's life. If he had devoted himself to Christ's service earlier, he would have achieved so much more; if he had been more disciplined, he would have lived longer; if he had resisted his temptations, he would have hurt others less. Yet if these things had been so, he would not have been George Burton.

He evoked strong reactions in all who met him: admiration, affection and loyalty; hostility, disgust and fear. The following pages are an attempt to capture something of all these aspects of his complex personality. Many issues are raised, social, psychological and spiritual, which need to be faced even if they can never be resolved. George Burton was a battle-ground for good and evil, and in recording some of the evil we do not wish to condone it, but rather to demonstrate that "where sin abounded, grace did much more abound".

Part One

PREPARATION (1915 –1958)

CHAPTER 1

Glasgow Boy

It was break-time at St. David's school, Glasgow, and the playground was alive with running, shouting, fighting children. A sturdy, keen-eyed eleven year old stood apart, his fresh-shorn head, from which a tuft of ginger hair stuck out, emphasised his large ears. His navy blue trousers and pullover and heavy boots marked out George Burton as a boy on parish relief. He was staring enviously through the iron railings which separated him from the children of an adjoining school. Their mothers were busily passing them flasks of tea, cakes and extra clothing, symbols of a wealth his family lacked.

It was 1926 and rations were short. Unemployment was widespread and Mr. Burton had been out of work since coming out of the British Army a few years previously. The family's poverty would prevent George from ever attending the school beyond the railings. A sense of injustice burned inside him as the bell recalled him to his lessons. The day dragged on, relieved only by the unsavoury dinner of lentil soup, and the smart of the strap on his hands from his hated teacher. When the afternoon bell finally released the children, George and his mates ran home along wide cobbled streets flanked with high tenements.

Number 4, Murray Street was the family's first home since coming to Glasgow from Ireland when George was a baby, and although the block had been condemned for the past ten years, their 'room and kitchen' was a great improvement on the accommodation they had been forced to share with other families when they first came to the city. George pushed the door open and ran in to his mother who listened sympathetically to the story of the strapping. In her ample embrace he felt secure, loved and wanted.

Alice Burton, of impressive stature, was a known character in Townhead. Having genteel connections in Dublin, she had seen better days. Outside her home she always wore a black hat and, instead of the common shawl, a long dark coat which distinguished her as a lady. She had reared her quiverful with the gaiety and courage born of hardship. Tom, the eldest, was a clever conversationalist and, being politically-minded, seemed set for a fine career. George, his hero worshipper, believed he could have entered Parliament; but he settled as a semi-skilled labourer. Lily was already married and living in Ireland by the time the family came to Murray Street. Bob had recently emigrated to Canada.

Kathy came next. Well-proportioned like her mother and wearing her dark hair in plaits, she was an ardent Salvationist. She enlisted 'wee Georgie' when he was seven and dressed him up in the red jersey to accompany her on pub rounds. While she went in complete with bonnet and tambourine to sell *The War Cry*, and face the showers of beer which were tossed at her, George would stay outside and watch the children waiting for their parents. He was shocked at the sight of drunken men holding small children in their arms and feeding them with fish and chips. Once the Lieutenant invited Kathy and George to tea in her home where they sat by her gas fire toasting buns and spreading them with real butter, a luxury unknown to the Burtons.

Polly was the youngest daughter, but by her teens she had returned to Ireland to be brought up by Mrs. Burton's mother, Granny Lambert. Last came 'wee Georgie'. When he was six George was told that a baby brother had been 'brought in the doctor's black bag'. But his joy was short-lived, for a few days later Polly and he returning from school were stopped outside their flat and sent to stay with the family upstairs. George was told that the doctor had taken the baby back again, but in his child's mind he blamed his father for Samuel's death.

Henry Burton was of heavier build but of less strong character than his wife. Yet he was genial enough and ready to do a good turn. He once helped a neighbour, Jessie Farrell, to varnish some furniture. Later that afternoon Jessie's father brought a guest home to tea, but as the visitor rose to go, his chair rose with him. Henry Burton passed his time mainly on the street corners and, when he could afford it, would place a penny or twopenny double with the local bookmaker. Drinking was a habit which he eschewed. As a soldier he had drunk heavily, sending his wife to the pub to fetch him a jug of beer. But he was jolted into signing the pledge and the whole family marched along to join the Tontine Lodge of the Good Templars. Thereafter Mrs. Burton would lead a brood of children to the upstairs room where they sang hymns, learnt anti-drink texts and were rewarded with cups of tea. George became chairman of the Lodge's juvenile section and his friends placed a sharp tack on his chair to deflate him after his inaugural speech.

Alice Burton had to support the home by cleaning a grocer's shop. She worked wonders of economy, sending George to fill their own tin with twopence worth of black treacle and using condensed milk or dripping as a change from the scrape of margarine. Porridge was the staple diet, with soup or pease broth at mid-day. It was a special treat when his mother called down to him in the street below, "Georgie, come and have the top of your father's egg."

The table cloth was kept for Sundays and pointed to a good meal, which Henry Burton would acknowledge with the words:

> "Thanks be to God for what we have had,
> If there was more, more we would have had.
> But seeing as the times they are so bad,
> Thanks be to God for what we have had."

The Burtons' best clothes normally resided at the pawn shop, to be taken out only at weekends. George thought wistfully of the only new pair of boots he ever remembered. Henry Burton had won on the horses and generously took George along Parliamentary Road to choose them; but they were hardly ever worn, for if he had played football in them he would have reduced their value. One Friday there was no money to redeem the boots, and George saw them no more.

It was a major operation to wash the family's clothes in the communal washhouse out in the courtyard. Attached to the washhouse was a dustbin recess, known as the 'midden'. But refuse did not always reach the bins, for it was more quickly disposed of by being flung straight out of the window into the courtyard below. This emboldened foraging rats to enter the apartments as well and most children in Murray Street were familiar with the pests.

Whatever other bills were left on one side the weekly penny for the life insurance policy had to be dug out, for everyone dreaded a parish burial. Another threat hanging over the home was removal to the poorhouse.

The Parish held an annual Necessitous Children's Camp and George enjoyed these rare excursions from the city. But the children were issued with a special uniform, and a 'tinny' (tin mug) was tied to their coat lapels, so that George never forgot this indignity which branded him as a slum child. His only other holidays away were when Granny Lambert sent him the fare and he visited his well-to-do relations in Dublin. The contrast between their way of life and his own endorsed his sense of inferiority. He disliked Christmas time for it only spot-lighted the family's straits. He consoled himself with gazing through the shop window at a magnificent grey fort complete with battlements and drawbridge and imagining that it was his own.

George belonged to a small gang, most of whose members lived around Murray Street and were older than him. Big Robbie Muirhead was the leader until he went to sea, when Harry 'Flash' Farrell took over. Bertie Thoms was something of a genius; he could make radio sets which really worked. Bimbo was tough as tanned leather. Any of them could wallop him with a shoe, at which he would laugh and ask for more. He was not altogether stupid though, for he would charge each of the others a halfpenny to watch him eat spiders' legs. They could not wholly accept into their circle a boy who was the son of a policeman. Then there was Albert Easdale who lived next door to the Burtons and whose father kept a shop. One of them would go in and say, "I want a pennyworth from that bottle up there," pointing to one on the highest shelf. While the shopkeeper's back was turned the others would nip in and help themselves.

Most of their games cost only toughness and daring. They would leap on to the side or back of travelling lorries. Many a boy missed his hold and injured himself in falling. Then they would chase each other along the road in front of a fruit and vegetable shop. While the first runners 'accidentally' knocked over some barrels, the others, following quickly behind, snatched up what they could. In the backyard they examined their haul, and cooked it over a fire in the washhouse. Once they broke into a tobacconist's and were dividing their spoil in the darkness of the 'dunny' (the alleyway leading from the staircase to the courtyard) when Mr. Burton, making one of his rare appearances, caught them red-handed and soundly thrashed his son.

In summer the gang went barefoot and loved to run behind the water-cart which sprayed the road. A three foot high pump was another source of amusement. George was once held under it to be baptised 'Paddy', for he still spoke with his parents' Irish brogue; though later in life he passed himself off as a Glaswegian.

To acquire any pocket money the boys had to use their wits. Two empty bottles earned a penny, for which they could enter the Grafton cinema which abutted on 4, Murray Street. The cinema roof became the gang's rendezvous, giving both security from police and an ideal vantage point. On sunny days they would strip, sunbathe and smoke. Five 'Frigates' cost only a penny and most of them took up smoking at eight or nine. They could all play cards too: rummy, brag, solo, even pontoon. While George could stand up for himself if necessary, he was content to leave others to display physical prowess, but cards was a sphere in which he could excel. Flipping and fingering them ceaselessly he began to pick up some tricks.

Townhead could boast churches and mission halls in profusion. Opposite the Burton home stood MacLeod Parish Church, but Mrs. Burton chose to attend the more fashionable Barony Church. George and his friends became connoisseurs of the various missions. The Band of Hope specialised in lantern slide lectures, after which came the welcome free tea and a bun. The magic lantern also featured at Mr. Thompson's Sunday School in the Gospel Hall, and lights out was the signal for children to make mischief. But Mr. Thompson was concerned for the youngsters and even invited them to his suburban home, collecting them and paying their tram fares. Once or twice George attended the Spiritualist Hall, known to the irreverent as the 'spooks church', but he remained sceptical and unconvinced by their claims.

Townhead was by no means the roughest area in Glasgow. A few minutes' walk from Murray Street stood St. Luke's Episcopalian Church which supported both a football team and a paid, surpliced choir. Accordingly George became a member of that choir, to which he contributed volume if not tone.

But it was the Life Boys which really gripped George and he joined the 169 Company, whose reputation was second to none in Glasgow. Bobby Ramsey, the young officer in charge, regarded it as a challenge to work in the Townhead district. His fiancée taught hand work, but George preferred the drill, games and hymn singing. With heart and soul he roared, 'Yield not to temptation', 'Courage, brother' or 'Onward Christian Soldiers'. Above all he was keen to wear the uniform, the sailor hat and sweater which Mr. Ramsey discreetly provided for boys who could not afford to buy them. The uniform was a badge of respectability and his mother always ensured that he left home tidy. Each month he would proudly take his place at the Sunday Parade and, with all eyes upon him, march through the streets to the church service.

The year's highlight was the company inspection. One year they had been practising for a display of Scottish dances and George was one of eight boys chosen to take part in the 'Triumph'. He urged his mother and sisters to come and see him, and a buzz of chatter heralded the start of the show. Mr. Ramsey swelled with pride as he watched the boys. 'The Triumph' started well, but suddenly Ramsey blinked, unbelieving, aghast. George Burton was performing a dance of his own design. With wild frenzy he flung arms and legs into a crazy jig quite unrelated to the steps he had learnt. Ramsey felt murderous, his whole season's work ruined. "George Burton," he hissed, "just let me get hold of you and . . ." But the hall was in an uproar of delight. Bobby Ramsey was relieved when George was twelve and moved up to the Boys' Brigade.

In January 1928 George was transferred to Townhead Public School, a red-brick structure holding 1,350 boys and girls in classes of up to sixty. A few hundred yards from the school gates stood the great cathedral of St. Mungo, opposite the Necropolis where Glasgow worthies lay buried. Such monuments meant nothing to George. Discipline was stern and the strap was used frequently. But Miss 'Studs' Struthers was easily evaded; you could jerk your hand away so that she strapped herself instead.

Truancy was rife, but after nearly eighteen months George's attendance record was well above average. He had acquired the ability if not the interest for reading, and for the next thirty years the world of books remained closed to him. He could write well enough, in a legible sloping script. But arithmetic was his best subject and he could work out difficult sums in his head. Nature study was his pet aversion for he still associated it with the teacher's strap.

Summer weekends saw the gang camping out at Bishopbriggs or Cadder Woods. For tents, a piece of old sacking; for food, each one contributed a little, supplemented by vegetables dug from fields' edges. At Busby Dam they went swimming, without trunks. Then they would organize boxing bouts at which 'Flash' Farrell fancied himself as champion, while George banged the frying-pan gong. The Bluebell Wood was the resort of love makers. "How many bluebells did you pick?" was understood to mean, "How did you get on with your girl?"

In their last year or two at school many boys took a job as lather boy in a barber's shop or with a bundle of papers on the street corner would cry '*Times*, *News* and *Citizen*'. George took on a milk and a paper round. By the time they left school George and his friends tracked down the colourful world of the amusements. But to George the appeal of the dance halls was the strongest. With his poise and fine sense of rhythm he excelled at dancing and discovered that his easy charm and flattery could win him the admiration of girls.

Whenever he ventured outside Townhead he went with his mates, but even they could not guarantee protection. During a dance in one of the roughest areas the atmosphere became dangerous. Most of the Murray Street set slipped out down a staircase to the back court. George was too late and became isolated. Before he could escape he was on the floor being kicked viciously from all sides and it was only the intervention of an older friend that saved him from worse injury than cuts and bruises. He could not pretend to his mother that he had been to the Boys' Brigade on *that* evening.

At every level the chief excuse for gang fighting sprang from religious bigotry.

> "A Billy or a Dan,
> Or an auld tin can?"

To this challenge Protestants replied 'Billy', Catholics 'Dan' and the let-out for non-fighters was 'auld tin can'.

Scores of voluntary agencies attempted to direct the young

people's energy towards sport. Many of them were inspired by evangelistic zeal and George began to hunger for the personal faith which they commended. He asked his friend Albert Easdale to take him to the Elgin Place Mission. Albert could hardly conceal his embarrassment at George's request. Better off than the others and always well-dressed, his standing at the Mission would hardly be improved by George's company. However he agreed to conduct George there one Sunday evening.

The service was bright, informal and sincere. The minister spoke about Jesus Christ who came to rescue lost boys and girls. The Son of God died for them, no matter how bad they were, taking on Himself the punishment for their sins. George rose to sing: "There is a fountain filled with blood." He realised that somehow through the death of Jesus he too could lose his guilty stains. Blinded with tears he joined in the chorus:

> "I do believe, I will believe
> That Jesus died for me,
> That on the cross He shed his blood
> From sin to set me free."

For several weeks afterwards he threw himself into the Mission's open-air services. He even dreamt that one day he might run a mission hall himself. At the same time he began to take notice of an attractive girl at the Mission. "I'd like to walk Anne home," he confided to Albert. "Do you think she'd let me?" Albert expressed grave doubts. It was true that Anne was a Christian, but she was also neat and tidy. "Look at your patched trousers, George, and the holes in your socks. She wouldn't want to go out with you." "If that's Christianity, it's not for me!" he retorted, and never went to the Mission again. Yet his spiritual experience was ineradicable.

He continued to lead a Jekyll and Hyde existence. He stayed a member of the Boys' Brigade; but no sooner was he out of the house than he tucked his pill-box hat into a niche of the dunny, and slipped off with the gang. When the Captain called to report his absences, Mrs. Burton guessed. "The young rascal, he's away with company."

Howbeit, his association with the 'B.B.' secured him his first job on leaving school and he was picked out of thirty applicants for a post in a store. He began by delivering goods to other shops and cleaning the office. Then he was trusted with petty cash and stamps. He made friends with the lift boy, and together they plotted that 'Lightning' would whistle a warning whenever the storeman of the nearest office used the lift. Then George would sneak in to steal a few cosmetics, and they shared the spoils to feed the fruit machines.

One evening at the amusements George met an older boy who was planning to run away to sea. George's imagination was stirred and he carried out a final theft to pay for the adventure. They took a train southwards and slept rough. Next day they reached Richmond in Yorkshire and applied to the Green Howards Regiment. George was accepted but decided to stick with his friend who was turned down on medical grounds. Later a policeman stopped them. His search revealed the stolen goods and the boys were brought before the court for young offenders. On hearing their story and confession of guilt the board of kindly old people collected the money for their rail fares and saw them placed under the care of the guard on the next train to Glasgow. George was deeply impressed by being given another chance.

His homecoming was happy too; for the lost son was given the assurance of being missed and wanted. And when his mother escorted him back to the office the manager congratulated him on not stealing any money and actually offered him a 2.6d. rise.

Yet the wanderlust remained. The Army uniform had appealed to George, and had he not passed the interview? Then the Army Recruiting Office notice caught his eye, and with calm decisiveness he announced, "I want to join the Green Howards." "How old are you?" the sergeant-major eyed him suspiciously. Confidently he lied, "Seventeen" (the minimum age for enlistment), and the interview was over. George was told to report to Richmond.

In the morning he waited for his father to leave home before breaking the news to his mother. She nearly fainted, but her pleas could not dissuade him. An hour later she and his sister Kathy wept for 'wee Georgie' as they waved the train out of sight.

CHAPTER 2

Soldier in India

The boy of fifteen, whose voice was only beginning to break, was awed by the solid bleakness of the parade ground at Richmond Barracks stretching out in front of him. Frowning over it stood the gaunt, grey barrack room where he was to eat, sleep and live for four months. His Geordie companions also seemed strange; for the Green Howards drew their recruits mainly from the north-east of England.

It was January 1931 and George had enlisted for seven years' service. Vast though they were, the quarters seemed to him quite agreeable, the food was sufficient and two shillings a day was good money. At first he avoided notice and observed quietly in order to trim himself into shape. The Boys' Brigade had already instilled ideas of tidiness and discipline, and so he worked eagerly at drill. It was the schooling which tripped him up. The Army Certificate of Education, Third Class, required elementary English which a ten year old could write. George passed, but only at the third attempt.

He spent a short leave in the home of a fellow-soldier. Some rowdy behaviour at table led to his knocking the salt cellar on to the floor; and for that he was turned out of the house. But it had been an accident and not a deliberate act, and a sense of grievance stayed with him. On his first leave home the lustre which came from showing off his new uniform was dimmed when his mother found in a pocket some sordid picture postcards. She rebuked her son loudly and publicly. And even his uniform was not respected by all. Whereas one girl was proud to press his trousers, another would not consent to be taken out by him until he had shed the uniform and borrowed a suit.

Moving to Aldershot he grew in self-confidence. Compared with his rather dour and taciturn comrades the Glasgow boy was lively and witty. He incurred the sergeant-major's anger by wearing his hat at a rakish angle. In an attempt to cover up his youthfulness he asserted himself as a 'barrack-room lawyer', adding to his sharp and argumentative nature a knowledge of legal technicalities. His wrangling won him a few friends and many enemies. By standing up for the rights of the ordinary soldier he became unpopular with the non-commissioned officers, and by his quickness at reporting any irregularity among his fellows he earned their ill-will too. His alertness made him a suitable candidate for the Signals and Intelligence sections; and he completed a draughtsmanship and a cook's course. He also doffed his cap at religion by taking a passing interest in a new movement called the Oxford Group.

By the time he sailed to India he was bearing the marks of manhood. The face was thinner, the forehead was creased in a puzzled frown, and a cigarette hung from his lips. Most of his five years in India were spent at Meerut.

A soldier's life was monotonous to the point of despair. The people, inspired by Gandhi, were chafing against British rule and appeared sullen most of the time. Occasionally the friction between Hindus and Muslims sparked off a riot; but otherwise there was no action. George succumbed to a severe bout of malaria from which three of his comrades died. Their hardships drew the men closer together. They 'mucked in' and shared everything; even their pay went into a common pool. George was a keen, smart soldier and a good 'mucker'. He went with everyone else to the cinema, played billiards, smoked more cigarettes than anyone and whiled away many secret hours at cards, a forbidden practice. The Sandes Soldiers' Home brought back a flavour of mission hall days, and he combined with these activities the duties of padre's orderly. Experience taught him to suppress his hot temper and litigiousness, and he devoted himself to organising sports and football matches, contriving to appear in the centre of every photograph.

George Burton was used to being in the minority. His family had been Protestants in Catholic Ireland, then Irish in Glasgow. He himself was no athlete and was also marked out by not drinking. These factors contributed to his enigmatical reserve, as if he were biding his time before disclosing his full personality. All the time he acted as if in disguise. This mysterious quality came to the surface in two conflicting ways.

On the one hand he was a total abstainer. This cut him off from a large section of social life; for most of the soldiers drank heavily. At Aldershot he had followed the fad of having his arm tattooed, and he chose the single word 'Mother' as a seal on the promise he had made to her not to drink. In India he was zealous enough to form a Good Templar Lodge, which brought him a congratulatory epistle in purest copperplate script from Glasgow's Tontine Lodge secretary.

> "It has been a revelation to our members to learn that you have the proud distinction of promoting and establishing a Good Templar Lodge within the regiment when you are only a private soldier.
>
> "Our members are profuse, in their congratulations, which are now being extended to you, in your wonderful achievement."

He added that the news had inspired Mrs. Burton to rejoin the Lodge.

> "and before very long, we all are hoping to have your father back with us, as in days gone and past. Meantime, I can only wish you God's speed in your devotion, and that you will long be spared to continue on in doing so, in such a great Cause."

In contrast to this virtuous stand against drink George made no secret of his sexual exploits and boasted of his success with white women; whereas some of his fellow-soldiers settled for low-caste Indian prostitutes.

In 1936 there was an uprising on the North-west Frontier and 130 soldiers were killed by Pathan tribesmen. George was posted to the garrison town of Razmak, a military monastery housing soldiers, mules and guns, surrounded by a jagged wilderness of rocks and thorn scrub, split by stony water-courses. The troops made expeditions from Razmak to pin down the elusive tribesmen who promptly vanished, blending into the background, and reappeared to strike down an unwary soldier. There were 'long slow days, sudden, quick minutes'. George had the sinew to survive and from Razmak he learnt to be wakeful, tense and ruthless. He also proved himself not only a capable signaller but calm and resourceful in a crisis.

In January 1938, at the age of nearly twenty-three, George had completed his seven years' service and was due to be discharged. A senior officer wrote of him: "Many hardships had to be endured. Private Burton did not fail and we are sorry to lose him from the Regiment. I can thoroughly recommend him." On the boat home he played crown and anchor with some sailors and lost his savings. So he coolly borrowed the board for the last night and won back thirty pounds, thus confirming another treasured testimonial: "He is above average intelligence."

CHAPTER 3

Palestine Police

Glasgow was still drab and struggling, even if the poverty was less crushing; but surprisingly George stayed there for six restless months. He fancied that his ready tongue and pleasing manner might fit him for salesmanship and tried selling 'Kleen-e-zee Brushes'.

The street gangs held little attraction for him and he recoiled on seeing his old friend Willy jerk a sharp tin edge across another man's face. Turning to the Boys' Brigade he was accepted as handyman at their Kilmacolm summer camp.

By that time May had entered his life. A part of George wanted to settle in a steady job and with the right wife, and his love for May was red hot. True, she came from a smarter district, but there was much about George to commend him. He toiled at a letter telling of his passion and waited on tenterhooks for her reply. Back it came: his letter was merely returned decorated with red correction marks. The intention may have been innocent, the effect was devastating. He interpreted it as a rejection not just of his bad English but of his humble background and of himself. He concealed the hurt and outwardly submitted to her tutorship. But the seed of a phobia took root in his mind, and in subsequent years it developed into a sense of panic when confronted by the need to write.

Soon after that he was attracted by a poster, "Join the Palestine Police and have a *Man's* job". Yes, he'd show everyone he was a man. After recent disturbances the British Government were recruiting a thousand police to undertake the frustrating duty under the mandate of protecting Arabs and Jews from each other, of upholding law and order in a country where everyone was a law unto himself. George had no secondary school certificate, but his military experience and ability to handle a gun secured his place. The man who sailed to Palestine in September 1938 was grimly resolved to conquer the handicap of his background. His staring eyes spoke of aggressiveness and ferocious determination.

He skipped through the early training and in one year passed the police exams which opened the door to possible promotion. "By no means a small achievement," wrote a senior officer. For George Burton it was astounding. Later he passed regular Arabic and the colloquial part of the Government exam in Arabic. He liked the Arabs and learnt more Arabic direct from them than from books. When spurred by a strong enough incentive he could write without difficulty, but otherwise found himself making excuses not to write more than necessary. Being a strict teetotaller and a church-goer George kept rather aloof from other policemen, and even in his spare time worked hard at his career.

At the outbreak of war many policemen were gibed at for remaining in civilian duties. Most begged to return to England and join up, but were not allowed to leave as the Police Force had been placed under the command of the G.O.C., Middle East Forces; and in fact they were more stretched and saw more action in Palestine than many of their countrymen in the fighting forces.

George's first posting was to the port of Haifa. Jewish immigrants from Europe were pouring through Haifa, many of them illegally, on their way to one of the settlements. There too the Jewish terrorist organisations were being formed to counter-attack the Arabs, and then to harass the British as well, when in 1939 the idea of an independent Jewish state being established in Palestine was quashed.

But George was concerned more with the routine offences of peacetime: loitering, housebreaking, assault and opium smuggling. P.C. 177 was made a contravention officer and became adept at ferreting out mail which had been sent from Jerusalem by taxi and bus to sidestep Post Office expenses. Once when he made a charge his senior told him that it was not worth prosecuting, at which he archly spread the matter before the Superintendent of Prosecutions, who gave him special permission to prosecute in the Chief Magistrate's Court. Although he was reprimanded for putting a leading question in examination, the young 'barrack-room lawyer' won his case.

His desire for female company led George into trouble with a married port official, but that was not the only reason he left Haifa.

He wanted to marry a Christian Arab girl. One of his seniors pointed out that he was not yet able to support a wife and anyway would not be allowed to marry until he had completed three years' service. Besides, a policeman who married an Arab or Jewess could be ostracised by his fellows, denied married quarters, and his prospects of promotion seriously impaired. The best solution was for him to be transferred; and so in the middle of 1940 he went to Hebron.

His few months there were marred by the loss of his rifle. One night he failed to keep it chained to his bed and it was stolen. Loss of firearms was a serious offence, for they could reach the hands of terrorists. Only his past record and church connections saved him from being dismissed from the force. Instead he was fined and his chances of promotion prejudiced. Later, when the rifle was recovered, George persuaded the authorities to erase the charge from their records.

At weekends he went into Jerusalem where the air was cooler and there was pleasant company at St. Andrews, the Church of Scotland. In that circle he was welcomed without being expected to drink and he enjoyed the social activities. During the sermon his attention wandered, absorbed by a trim, petite figure. "Good morning," he greeted her after the service. "Good morning," she replied in faltering English. And that was all.

Early in 1941 George obtained a transfer to the police station in the German Colony, the fashionable southern suburb of Jerusalem. And the foreign lady whom he had admired lived only a few doors away from his billet. "This must have been arranged for me," he mused. All through his life he remained conscious that each event was directed by God and filled with special significance for himself.

One Sunday he remarked to the young lady, whose name was Helena, "That was a good sermon." As she did not appear to understand he explained his meaning. He was nervous at first, for Helena was dainty and refined, and etiquette did not come naturally to him. The next stage was an invitation to tea, at which a chaperon was present. At length George's charm conquered, the chaperon withdrew and they went out together.

Helena came from a middle–class Hungarian family and her father was a Government official. Her mother was a German and her mother's great-uncle had been a general in the British Army. George was impressed that his name had a page in the *Dictionary of National Biography*. Helena was a high-class dressmaker with excellent qualifications and by dint of thrift and industry she had built up an enviable clientele. She was a person of good taste who loved to play Chopin and Liszt on the piano. Her sister Mariska had married a Russian-Jewish sculptor and Helena, after living with them in Tel Aviv, had rented a pleasant house in the German Colony, part of which she shared with Mariska and her husband.

Helena had lived a sheltered life and did not know English class prejudice. She gathered that George came from a humble home, but also that his mother was of good family and that his brother Tom might have become a Member of Parliament. More important, George himself was smart, straight-shouldered and personable, and set for a promising career.

The two were already engaged when, on Hungary's entry into the war, Helena became an alien and was due to be interned. George rose to the occasion, for he knew how to pull strings. He appealed to some influential friends to backdate his application for marriage and the wedding took place on December 22nd, 1941. But his marriage did not forward George's career. Some senior officers disapproved of his marrying one of the enemy, while others supposed that Helena was a Jewess. His promotion was delayed still longer and it was only with difficulty that George obtained permission to live with Helena.

The stone-built house was more charming than he could have dreamt about in 4, Murray Street. With attractive shutters, veranda and balcony it stood back from a quiet, broad avenue. Up the walls climbed yellow roses and the cool garden was shaded by almond trees. In the back garden a hundred chickens scratched away, while pigeons roosted in the loft. Their persistent cooing above the bedroom became irritating and George volunteered to clear the loft of the birds. But the chase ended when he slipped between the rafters and was suspended in mid-air, legs dangling helplessly, until Helena rescued him.

Their pleasant surroundings did not guarantee harmony, though the early days were marked by a degree of pleasure George had seldom known. Still a child at heart, he was seeking his mother's love. After work he would hurry indoors to recount the day's events to Helena, telling her not to interrupt his speech. He liked her to wash his hair and his back and would then appeal, "Do I smell nice?" When he was in a good mood his strident voice blared out his mother's favourite song, 'Clementine'. For the first few years their differences of temperament and outlook were submerged by outside interests. Helena was busy housekeeping and dressmaking and George's job still came first in his mind. He did shift work at the German Colony station, and so often slept by day. He spent many off-duty hours at St. Andrews and continued, though not so regularly, to attend the church services.

When the minister of St. Andrews opened a hostel he found in George a ready assistant and organiser. He was jovial and a good mixer, arranging whist drives and dances at which Helena would lend her support. He ran a Scottish football team which competed against police and forces teams. He himself never played but preferred, as manager, to organise others. For servicemen stationed in Jerusalem he led trips to the Biblical sites, though the places held little historical interest for him.

Their home became an extension of the social life of St. Andrews. Helena got used to groups of men and women from the forces being brought in by George unannounced and expecting meals, for which she had to enlist Mariska's help. One man was happy playing their piano until two in the morning. At Christmas time, as if to compensate for his childhood deprivations, George would surround himself with company and try to make the festival memorable for others.

George had already joined Dr. Weiser's bridge club where he met the cream of the German-Jewish intellectuals and picked up enough German to converse with them. The Attorney-General noticed him there and invited him to play bridge in his own home. Helena would sometimes come to watch and sip drinks, while George stuck to his pot of tea.

On his leaves George took Helena sightseeing. Once they toured Syria and Lebanon and saw the ruins of Baalbek; but usually they went to Egypt and did the rounds of the Sphinx, the Pyramids, and the Egyptian Museum in Cairo, consumed huge ices at Groppi's and visited the theatre. They both enjoyed the luxury of the Shepheard Hotel where George played bridge.

Other policemen did not see much of George and had no reason to suspect anything amiss in his marriage. He started to play chess but was a bad loser and gave it up. He was a fanatic at table tennis and gambled on every game. The influence of his neighbour Tommy Blount obtained for him a much envied job, permanent duty officer at the headquarters of the C.I.D.

In 1944 George was at last promoted to Second British Sergeant and posted to the country station of Nablus, an Arab area which had been turbulent before the war. They were offered married quarters, but as the post was only for a year, they decided that Helena should remain in Jerusalem to keep their house and her business, and George would return there at weekends. Sometimes she visited him in Nablus for a few days at a time.

In the rugged, stony district of Nablus, where olive trees grew and cicadas screeched, George came to know the Arabs better than ever before. His fluent Arabic and genial manner made him readily accepted. Sipping small cups of bitter coffee he listened while they lectured him about the Palestine problem. Normally inert they became fierce with indignation as they listed their injuries. George nodded and kept a discreet silence. Like many British policemen he sympathised with them, and more so as the Jewish terrorists increased in violence.

Early in 1945 George was due four months' leave and wanted to take Helena to visit his mother in Glasgow. Helena, however, feared she would not be allowed to return to Jerusalem and pressed him to go alone. For three weeks George stayed with his mother and in the evenings they sat by the fire while she made toast for him. But he was so repelled by Glasgow that he curtailed his leave to return to Nablus. Within days a telegram informed him that his mother had died. His gratitude at having seen her in time was blemished by stabbing remorse. If only he had stayed on with her a bit longer, if only he had written more letters, if only he had cared more for her. Now that she was gone he felt empty and lost.

Towards the end of 1945 George was posted back to Jerusalem. The war was over and both Jews and Arabs were employing violence to force Britain's hand. The Administration had already lost the initiative and was unable to make firm decisions, so sabotage and murders increased. When the section of the King David Hotel which was used as the Police Secretariat was blown up with ninety-six casualties, George was on the other side of the road and was flung on to the ground by the force of the explosion.

A new unit called the Jerusalem Operational Patrols was formed to combat terrorism. George was in charge of one of its four sections of armoured cars which patrolled the city twenty-four hours a day. Later he was entrusted with the entire administration of J.O.P. His base was a large 'Ops Room' from which he was in touch by radio with all the cars. The walls were covered with huge charts on which every street in the city was marked, and he knew the exact position of each patrol car. He was an efficient administrator and justly proud of his empire which he readily showed to important visitors. Through J.O.P. he learnt the value of teamwork and of liaison with other branches like the army.

While others were itching to escape from the tension of being caught between two opposing forces, George revelled in the situation. It suited the complexity of his character. Whenever the siren sounded George was there imparting a calm air of authority to the crews under his control. His nerves appeared unaffected and when his senior officers showed signs of strain George would politely suggest that it was time for a cup of tea. On the other hand his chain smoking betrayed underlying nervousness and his habit of letting the ash drop over his uniform earned him the nickname 'Fag Ash'.

Even off duty George was always a policeman. He was once on his way with Helena to the cinema when they saw some fighting. Immediately George sent Helena home in a taxi while he dealt with the trouble.

In June 1947 George took another leave and this time Helena went with him to Glasgow. Their stay there was brief and Helena was not shown 4, Murray Street. She pined to see her own family in Budapest, and despite the post-war difficulties of such a visit, George directed his energy and resourcefulness to obtaining the necessary permits. An adventurous journey united Helena to her father and brothers whom George met for the first time. They then spent a week at the Grand Hotel, Karlsbad, in the company of an Indian Rajah.

Back in Palestine the two sides were preparing for battle and George threw himself again into J.O.P. He was interviewed for promotion to Inspector, but the Mandate was due to be terminated in May 1948 and the promotion was frozen. His thoughts were also occupied with his pension for which he would not qualify until September. Men in his position were given the opportunity of staying on in Palestine with a volunteer force of 500 to complete the full period for their pensions. George argued that by not returning to England straightaway he would miss the best openings for police in the Colonies. But Helena persuaded him to stay for the final few months, even though it meant that she had to leave and sail to England alone.

By that time the British troops and police, who were no longer responsible for the maintenance of law and order, withdrew into the Haifa Enclave leaving the combatants to fight it out. It was assumed that the Arabs' numerical superiority would overwhelm their opponents. Instead the Jews captured one town after another and George witnessed some 40,000 Arabs emigrating from Haifa alone.

In the previous year Helena's sister Mariska had married her second husband Peter. George, who had always had a soft spot for Mariska, had lent them money to open a café and pastry shop in the German Colony. Although life was hard, they chose to stay on in Jerusalem at the end of the Mandate. One day George, his face brick-red from the sun, arrived from Haifa with five other police officers, bringing provisions and £30. "However did you get here?" asked Mariska. "Shush, don't ask me," George whispered. "It was very difficult."

Meanwhile Helena wrote to George from London. "I had a miserable journey, everything here is dark and sad. I am feeling lonely. Why don't you write and send me some money? I want to go with you to Canada." George responded by sending her £60.

The police finished their work in Haifa early and George was back in England by July. One lesson imprinted on him was that in a many-sided situation it is not wise to be over rigid and abide always by the letter of the law. One has to be flexible enough to make exceptions. And so he left the Holy Land with its curious gleaming domes, the sun-drenched courtyards, the busy souqs, the dark alleys, the Muslim calls to prayer mingling with the crowing of cocks. These picturesque sights and the holy places themselves had formed a scarcely noticed background to his career as a policeman. During these years he had indeed realised many ambitions, and yet contentment eluded him.

CHAPTER 4

Benghazi

Helena watched proudly as, with others representing the Haifa Five Hundred, her husband marched to Buckingham Palace to be presented to H.M. King George VI. And George himself beamed when the King spoke to him personally. He had turned down a commission with the police in Malaya and was able to fill the final two months for his pension working at a spacious country house in Hertfordshire, where the affairs of the Palestine Police Force were being wound up. At the age of thirty-three he was already a pensioned police officer and after Palestine whatever he did next was bound to be an anti-climax.

In December 1948 George was offered the post of Assistant Establishment Officer to the British Military Administration of Cyrenaica. He had been interviewed for the job back in Palestine and had learnt that Britain had taken over Cyrenaica from Italy and was to administer the country until it was ready for independence. His job would be administrative and would involve correspondence. He flinched from it, conscious of his difficulty of writing. He confided his misgivings to his former neighbour Tommy Blount who assured him that he would manage provided that he could delegate, and recommended his taking a correspondence course in English.

Wives were expected to join their husbands later, so Helena remained for the present in the rooms in Kensington where she had been living for the past few months. George left England alone shortly before Christmas. Benghazi was pock-marked from the War, its white geometrical buildings huddling together beneath the palms with an air of bereavement. Around the harbour pieces of iron rusted, while the rains were turning the red soil into a quagmire. A sense of foreboding descended on George.

He discovered that out of the several ex-Palestine policemen sent to Benghazi he alone had been appointed an officer in the Secretariat. The others, even ex-Inspectors, were drafted into more practical work in the transport or harbour sections. George was shown his apartments in the officers' quarters complete with his own servant.

Having climbed so high he felt dizzily inadequate. He could check and file; but writing and dictating letters, that was another matter. He shuddered at the thought of people sneering at his bad English. Yes, he had foolishly overreached himself. He remembered the false pose he had adopted at his interview in order to secure the job. And now he was caught in a trap which he himself had set. His own pride blocked the escape. Better the sweaty jumpiness of Jerusalem Operational Patrols than the awesome dignity of that office. Nervously he picked up a pen from the huge desk—and put it down. He went out for a cup of tea.

On his first day at work he was taken ill and admitted to hospital. The diagnosis was clear to him alone and he was discharged back to work. A chain of letters came from Helena in London.

"What happened? Did you have a cold? Did you eat something unclean? Please be careful. You need someone beside you who takes care of you. Perhaps you don't sleep enough. Perhaps it was the result of my bad dream about you. I dreamt that we wanted to go somewhere by train but we were always delayed.

"It will be nice to have a home and be together again, and I hope a better understanding will be between us.

"Mariska and Peter cannot stay in Jerusalem, there is no future for them. Please help them to get out. Please inquire if they can come to Cyrenaica."

He mentioned to her his writing difficulty and she tried to encourage him.

"Don't be afraid about your work; you have some friends. I wouldn't be ashamed to ask them and they will help you, or you will find someone to teach you to write letters. Once upon a time they didn't know how to write a letter. Just a little patience and you shall know it too. To learn is not a shame."

But in George's mind the problem was not so simple. How could the Assistant Establishment Officer admit he could not write English? The whole of Benghazi would roar with laughter. Yet the need was so pressing that he confided a measure of his inadequacy to two colleagues. They helped him to tackle his correspondence, which covered dental treatment and blood doning, an athletics meeting and public holidays. After the day's work he crept back to the office and furtively copied out ponderous bureaucratic expressions from letters in the files, and then learnt them by heart. Conscientious by nature, he was extremely sensitive about writing correctly. The strain was tremendous and he later described it as "hours and hours of fear".

In the spring George took Tommy Blount's advice and registered himself for a correspondence course in elementary English. His writing did develop, though he never achieved more than a pedantic woodenness. He dithered over whether to use the preposition 'with' or 'to', and dropped out before the final exam. An essay which he wrote on 'Winter' disclosed how childhood poverty was carved on his mind. "Winter to some people means sport and a good time, to others it means misery and unhappiness. Poor people who are not in the position to buy warmer clothing or fuel to keep a fire going usually feel miserable during the winter."

Helena came in April, one of the pleasantest months in Benghazi, and they were given a six-roomed flat overlooking the harbour with a view of the boats and the palms along the waterfront and the climbing bougainvillaea. She loved riding in the horse-drawn gharries, and even George admitted a liking for the flamingoes on the lagoon. They attended the Scottish services and Helena played the piano; but the spirit of St. Andrews was lacking.

British society in Benghazi was sufficiently small and exclusive for George to feel self-conscious and unsure of himself. By becoming an officer in Government Service he had crossed from one of Us to one of Them. His former seniors in Palestine were barred from the select Officers' Club to which he was now entitled to go. He was proud to take Helena there, but the main occupation of drinking repelled him. Part of him longed to mix with the Arab people, the peasants bringing their squawking hens into market, the droves of boys begging cigarettes. But that would not have been proper for the Assistant Establishment Officer. He felt he was only masquerading and dreaded the moment when someone would unmask him. His only release was in playing bridge with a small circle of acquaintances.

He found some relief in rising to a challenge set by Helena's relatives. She ached persistently with anxiety for Mariska who was still penned in Israeli Jerusalem, so George agreed to devote three weeks' leave to visiting her. Their scheme however reached the ears of the Egyptian Consul in Benghazi who thought Helena was a Jewess, and as they stepped out of the plane at Cairo they were arrested. After being detained in a hotel for three days George pulled strings to gain their release. On reaching the Arab side of Jerusalem they were told firmly that only United Nations officials and the Consulate were permitted to cross the 'no man's land' at the Mandelbaum gate. Doggedly George probed security officers whom he knew. Interviews were arranged, phone calls were made and permission was finally given just for Helena to see Mariska for not more than ten minutes in the middle of no man's land. George was left standing by holding a parcel of fruit and eggs. Suddenly he tore past the guard, the guns trained on his back, to join Helena and Mariska and to deliver his parcel. Somehow they returned unscathed to Benghazi.

But for George the tension continued and he snapped. Helena was the tormented victim of his sickness. In November 1949, before completing his year's contract, he left abruptly on the pretext that he was going ahead to seek out a home for them in England.

CHAPTER 5

London Life

It was well into February before Helena finally managed to leave Benghazi. She wanted to return via Jerusalem to see her sister, but needed George to arrange for her visa to London. Not unnaturally she chivvied him about this, and about finding a tutor for his English studies, about his food and laundering and keeping warm.

Meanwhile George had gone to ground in Glasgow, staying with his sister Kathy and experiencing what she termed a 'brainstorm'. He had escaped from a situation which was crushing him, but was still haunted by the horror of his failure. He reasoned that he should never have tried to better himself by leaving Glasgow, for he was only fit to be a labourer. "I'm nothing but a wash-out," he kept repeating as he wandered through the Glasgow streets. He walked by St. David's school and there came back to him the lentil soup and the strap, the parish uniform and the bare feet. Beyond the railings stood Provanside, the school to which he had been denied entry for lack of fifteen shillings a year. Murray Street had not changed and number 4 was still condemned. He recalled how in the evenings, when his father had gone to bed, his mother would make toast for him while he sat in the only armchair. His sense of guilt at having failed her overwhelmed him. How could he atone, now that she was gone? He had sacrificed £60 to provide a handsome gravestone, but that could not bring her back.

He might help to relieve poverty. As he watched some ragged children playing, a dream appeared before him: the washhouse in each courtyard being turned into small recreation centres and George Burton himself supervising the children's games. *That* was the way of atoning. He went up to the children and handed them some coins. They stared at him in disbelief, then ran off to spend the money in case he should demand it back. "May God be with all poor children," he sighed.

The dream passed and he slumped back into despair. He was adrift with no confidant to whom he could turn. Scared of suicide he bolted to London where his depression increased and he was admitted to hospital.

On discharge he took rooms in Robert Adam Street, off Baker Street, and turned to the only society where he could find diversion, the world of bridge. Here he could lose himself in complete absorption in the game. Here he could regain confidence in his ability to mix in high society. He adopted a public school accent and a quiet manner, and dressed immaculately. He played at night and slept by day.

Helena's arrival from Benghazi was an incidental interruption. After living with her for a short time he abandoned her once more. Dominated by a passion to conquer the very best bridge players, he joined one of London's leading clubs in Mayfair and worked his way up until he was playing for high stakes. Three of the top players would conspire to milk him. When he lost, they condoled with him, attributed his loss to bad luck and begged him to play another rubber. Strangely blind to their designs, his vanity tickled, he would welcome the opportunity to prove himself again. He played and lost frenziedly, sometimes £20 or £30 a night. He did not care so long as he belonged and was accepted. Neither a warning letter from Helena's only London friends reminding him of his responsibility towards her, nor the news that his bank balance was overdrawn, succeeded in abating his bridge fever.

Two weeks later he drained his savings and was bankrupt. In four months he had lost £2,000. The taste of honey swiftly passed and he was jolted back to the unbearable reality of failure and poverty. He was cornered. There seemed only one way out and he walked down into Tottenham Court Road tube station. Trembling at the brink near the tunnel he waited for the clatter of the next train. His jump was a fraction too late: he merely rebounded, and stumbled away in a daze. For several days he went hungry and without cigarettes, sharing morsels with the tramps in Hyde Park. He even turned to Helena, but she was in no mood to sympathise with him.

Then came the summons to answer the charge of desertion. With a surge of guilt-ridden despair he wandered through the open door of a church and up to the Holy Table where he threw himself down on the floor. "O God," he sobbed, "I've done wrong. I'm a filthy sinner. Please forgive me, forgive, forgive." He lay there a long time. Gradually it dawned on him that he himself could never succeed in atoning for the wrong he had done. God accepted him because Christ had done the atoning for him. George Burton left St. Paul's Church, Portman Square, knowing that he was a forgiven man.

Back at his digs was a letter, forwarded from Glasgow, calling him for an interview in London. It was assumed that he had travelled from Glasgow, so although he was not offered the job he was handed eight pounds expenses. Accepting the money as from heaven he bought a packet of cigarettes and a steak meal.

Within a week he found employment with Godfrey Davis, the car hire firm. Across the road from their offices stood the London City Mission, and for a moment he contemplated applying to them instead. But visions of running his own mission hall had to await fulfilment. He was given a clerk's job from five till ten each evening. He could manage the filing but was bewildered by the fractions and percentages required for the task of keeping accounts. His helplessness attracted the sympathy of Dick Brown, the telephone operator, who tutored him, gave him money and even lodged George in his own flat. Dick was a socialist with lofty ideals and burning social concern, and proceeded to woo George through books and argument. He was disappointed. George clung to the conforming conservatism which had suited him ever since, turning his back on Glasgow, he had aspired to higher social status. Though dependent on Dick, he struggled to assert his independence. He disputed the other's views, and, when defeated by logic, retaliated with outbursts of temper, even coming to blows. After each row George returned to implore pardon, and Dick, while despising him, was somehow prevailed upon to relent.

George was soon able to install himself again in Robert Adam Street and divided his life into unrelated compartments. At work he undertook to reorganise the files of check cards and managed to impress the chairman with his ability and industry. To those who knew him superficially he was pleasant and helpful, and he in turn blossomed in the comradely atmosphere of the office, where he stayed for three years.

4

He had not been at Godfrey Davis more than a month before he was hankering for a game of bridge. He joined a small private club where stakes were low and he could win more often than lose. Each night after work he would play for as long as he could persuade anyone to stay with him. Soon he was introduced to a set of titled people among whom he shone as a player so brightly as to be called 'the Maestro'. At the office he took delight in announcing, to Dick's disgust, that Lady X had just phoned inviting him to bridge. He had to demonstrate that he, George Burton, could both play bridge and mix in the highest society.

Besides work and bridge there was the third compartment for which George assumed yet another pose: religion. The incident in St. Paul's Church was an emotional burst of self-pity and self-despair, but it was more. He wanted God and yet he feared total engagement to God. He preferred to remain neutral and apply to God only when he needed help. After lingering on the edge of a small meeting in Oxford Street he disputed afterwards with the speaker. "Look at the Christians," he sneered, using ammunition given by Dick. "Christianity is just for respectable hypocrites, wealthy capitalists. The Church isn't interested in the working classes." The speaker, Roland, contrived to find a text to match the moment: "Man looketh on the outward appearance, but God looketh on the heart." As he reflected afterwards, the words pierced George's cynicism. "Yes," he thought, "God must see through my double-dealing." The steady sincerity of Roland attracted him. Later he learnt that Roland was a member of that same church, St. Paul's, Portman Square.

Next Sunday when George arrived late for the morning service he was asked to stay in the porch for a few moments. Furious at being kept waiting he tried to assault the sidesman, who hurriedly explained that the vicar, Prebendary Colin C. Kerr, was in the middle of saying prayers. After the service Roland approached George and introduced him to the curate, the Rev. Joe Mullins, whose genuine friendliness won George immediately. Mullins also lived in Robert Adam Street and kept tugging George into the church life. But there were no quick victories, for he was slippery and hot-tempered. Mullins and Roland never knew when he might appear, either during a church service or at their flats, seeking help for a personal problem. "I'm not a bad man," he insisted; and whenever they asked questions or passed judgement on him they did not see him again for a while. So they had to be patient and wait. Gingerly, incoherently, he began to confide in them, then listen to their advice, then pray with them about his problems. From them he learnt not only to pray aloud but also to expect results.

George started to parry Dick's thrusts by claiming that he was a Christian. He did indeed pay respect to high moral principles, but his beliefs were contradicted by his conduct. Dick was chiefly nauseated by George's relationships with women. Being a superb dancer, an amiable, almost charming conversationalist and possessing, despite his coarseness, a physical magnetism, George was a ladies' man. He had the ability to make a woman feel important and needed. Having won her affection and pity he would lean upon her for a time, then sadistically thrust her aside without any regard for the feelings which he had aroused. One claimed that he fathered her child, but although he acknowledged to Dick that the boy had his large ears he refused to accept responsibility, or help the mother. To him the matter was now closed. The callous way in which George described these affairs endorsed Dick's opinion that Christianity was a sham.

It was now more than a year since George had seen Helena and a court order bound him to pay her a weekly maintenance of thirty shillings. Arrears mounted and George was issued with a summons for their payment. He decided to frustrate the court order by obtaining a reconciliation. Helena, at first surprised, welcomed her husband's overtures and took a basement flat off Kensington High Street.

The old misunderstandings and irritations soon returned. Within a few days they quarrelled over the amount agreed upon for housekeeping. He still played bridge and went to his church; she still pursued her couture and went to her church. He had his circle of friends, she had hers.

During that summer of 1951 George's imagination became clouded with dark suspicions. He did not approve of Helena's female friends. He started to come home at unexpected times to eavesdrop and to spy on her from behind trees and corners. He scrutinised her mail, searching each letter for some secret code. The volcano burst one night when George set on Helena with a torrent of accusations. He was by now far deranged and she waited for her chance to escape. He returned from work to find the house empty and a note: "I feel very ill. I have left you." His morale crumbled. Suicide filled his thoughts and his doctor placed him under the care of a psychiatrist, Dr. Hunt.

It was to Joe Mullins from St. Paul's Church that he turned when he was summoned to answer the charge of persistent cruelty. Outside the court the two men paced up and down in the November cold, George quivering feverishly, while Joe, calm and steadying, urged him for honesty's sake to plead guilty and apply for God's forgiveness. Together they prayed and went inside. George found himself pleading guilty, while Helena, having agreed with her lawyer to claim a maintenance allowance, declared that she wanted nothing from him. Incredulously George came out muttering, "She didn't ask for a penny." Husband and wife were legally separated and hardly saw each other for another four years.

CHAPTER 6

Eva

George was being battered by the wildest storm of his life, a storm whipped up by his own fears and imaginings. God gave him, as he put it, a 'captain' and a 'mate' to guide his boat. The captain was Dr. Hunt. The mate was a girl in her twenties called Eva whom he met at a dance the day after the separation order. George suspiciously imagined that the two were accomplices associated with Dick Brown in a big communist network threatening to enmesh him.

With a theatre date and further meetings, George began to relax in Eva's company. She had a gay yet cultured beauty, fresh, open features and bright, sensitive eyes. Being adventurous she was drawn to this unusual man, so gifted and experienced, but so confused, helpless and dependent. Eva listened sympathetically as he revealed his background in a garrulous disorder. He told her of the broken marriage, of his childhood, his mother, his girl friends, the attempted suicide and his failure in Benghazi. At last he entrusted her with the deepest secret of all, his fear of writing. "Why don't you write to me, George?" she suggested casually as they parted one day.

Her challenge rang in his ears as he returned to his room. He seized a pen and started scribbling. "Please understand I am paying you the biggest compliment of my life by even writing a few words to you," he started. Then without stopping he covered fourteen pages in a large scrawl. This was his own writing and he had copied from no one. Hastily he posted his achievement to Eva and awaited her reaction in terror lest she should ridicule his mistakes. Next day he demanded the pages back and tore them to pieces before her eyes. Dutifully Eva pieced them together and urged him to write her some more.

For George this was an uncharted voyage which could only be undertaken with safety in Eva's company.

"Prior to my getting to know you I was not able to pick up a pen and I was very frightened even to write a few words to my near relatives.

"I know why I tore up those letters, because I was dreading the reading of them. You must have noticed how I never really get down to the study of grammar. Is it because I was a dunce at School and have not admitted it till recently. I hope that one day I will be able to write without grammatical mistakes. I suppose then I will have reached my 'utopia'."

Eva was the one person whom he could trust, yet even with her tuition he could not believe that success was within reach. He started each letter to her with the same formula, an apology for his bad English.

"I can see that I will never be able to master English. The actual writing is not difficult it is the finding of the words and sentences and the punctuating them is where the difficulty comes in."

Through the early months of 1952 the letters flowed. Eva's firm but tactful corrections and her affectionate interest stirred George to express himself on paper. She undertook to teach him grammar and set him paragraphs to punctuate and essays to write. He absorbed laboriously a lesson on the difference between the noun 'effect' and the verb 'affect'. Eva set him an examination paper, at the end of which he asked his tutor anxiously, "Would one get fifty per cent in an examination for it?" Eva's reply offered a ray of hope, "I think one might say fifty per cent (just)."

Hope was needed for George was tempted to despair.

"I have come to the conclusion that I will never be able to spot the difference between a verb and a noun. When I try to do them on my own I am completely lost. Is it because I have nothing to copy from? There must be some reason, for when you are with me you must admit I can pick them out.

"I well realise you have been nice to me so as to help me keep going. The engine is going at the moment and I pray that it won't conk out, if I hear a chugging sound I will go to 'Eva' who helped me get it started."

With Dr. Hunt's weekly sessions and Eva's steady friendship, George was beginning to unravel the twisted threads of his own personality.

"My dear Eva, I owe you my life. During the days that I first got to know you I only lasted out because I knew I was meeting you and you would let me speak to you. I owe you a lot for the fact that I am even attempting to write.

"It would be impossible to explain the feeling I have when I pick up the pen. Why should any grown person be frightened to write a few words? I suppose I am frightened that I spell the words wrongly and that I use words wrongly. Why am I not frightened of writing to you? Is it because I have told you so much or is it because I have got over the fear of writing a letter without copying.

"Nobody will ever be able to understand what I have gone through—mental anguish I suppose is the expression. I should have been locked up years ago."

Eva's acceptance of his early letters cushioned the painful crash he had feared.

"I think I have fallen off the precipice into the abyss," he wrote. "Obviously there was no bed of spikes otherwise I would have been badly injured and probably incapacitated from ever being able to write a stupid letter again. Seemingly my fall was broken by the sailors catching me in the tarpaulin—for I am on the boat at the moment—and I feel a bit sick—mind you—I am not as sick as I expected, as faith plays an important part in everything. I have great faith in the captain of the ship, Dr. Hunt, and his mate, Eva."

Dr. Hunt learnt of George's friendship with Eva and asked to see her. He warned that George could be violent and advised her to avoid meeting him when she sensed such a mood. But it was some months before she saw this side of his nature. At first she was aware only of his helplessness. He dreaded being left alone, especially at night, and she often waited until he was safely in bed and asleep before leaving him. At weekends she joined him in his rooms.

George had only recently attempted to drive, for it was his fixed notion that driving was the prerogative of the educated. Eva encouraged him to venture with her into the London traffic in a car borrowed from Godfrey Davis, and he had no scruples about tampering with the milometer. They drove also to Bedfordshire where she introduced him to her family, whom he held spellbound with his card tricks.

The experience of being wanted solely for himself was unfamiliar.

"My dear Eva, The first invitation I get to a home is from your mother. London with so many homes and families and I only get invitations to play bridge. I well know that my company is only desired by those people because I can handle fifty-two cards. Nobody has had any time for me and being honest I have only had time for myself.

"I well realise that if any of that crowd knew that I was from the slums of Glasgow they would not speak to me. I must inevitably face the fact that I have received a poor education, consequently I am not entitled to imagine myself better than those that I was brought up with. Admittedly I have tried to better myself, but I have bluffed my way through life."

In spite of his growing insight into his own needs, bridge continued to grip him, providing an escape from himself through the night hours.

"I have just returned from playing bridge and having made three beautiful psychic bids I am bursting with confidence of my ability to conquer the world—bridge world."

Throughout this period Glasgow was not far from his thoughts.

"Every day I fight the temptation to settle my difference with the slums of Glasgow," he confessed.

Eva made him promise not to return there without first telling her, and Dr. Hunt explained that to return would be to take the line of least resistance.

"I keep saying that I will probably lose my job because I argue with my bosses. I admit that the main reason is I am frightened of my inability to do my work. I am not cut out for office work.

I should have been a labourer. It is a pity that I ran away from Glasgow."

Reminiscing about his childhood he told her:

"It was the accepted fact that poor children came from poor parents and we had not the right to better ourselves. When we ventured down the main streets we automatically gave way to what we called our 'betters'.

"It is amazing the number of children who were kept off school because they had no change of clothes. I remember once just after I had been *issued* with a suit from the Education Authorities I got it soaking wet and we had to make a fire from the dross we had in the bunker to dry it before morning."

Dick Brown made him view the problem from a political angle.

"I do not blame God for those conditions but I do blame the Govt. that allowed them to exist. Poor children unless given the chance have really no way of developing their talents. An incentive must be created and something done to help them."

But there was also a Christian reason for combating social injustice.

"It is my contention that not enough is being done for the poor people, and I think that all politicians should read and practice what our Lord preached. The Sermon on the Mount should be practiced and I am sure it would be a better world."

He was not content merely to blame the politicians. He longed to do something himself.

"Do you believe that I want to run a club for poor boys or do you think I want to create an impression.

"My dear Eva, I have prayed to God and I still pray to Him that He will let me have my wish. I am now thirty-seven years of age and I am sure with His help when I am forty I will be able to open a club in the dirtiest and filthiest and slummiest and poorest place in London or Glasgow. I will do it. I have always wanted that since the day I ran away from home."

"Lord, help me to win the football pools," he prayed, as he filled in his weekly coupons, "and I will build you the biggest and best boys' club in Britain." He went so far as to visit some clubs, but their approach did not appeal to him, and for a time he showed no further interest.

Prebendary Colin Kerr, however, persuaded him to lend sporadic help with the Campaigners, a Christian uniformed youth movement, and in August 1952 he was asked to fill a vacancy as quartermaster at a camp in the Isle of Wight. Frank, the officer who called for him, found him half-dressed, smoking and red-eyed after an all-night bridge session.

Soon he was writing to Eva:

"I am enjoying myself. It has been after midnight the last 2 nights before getting into bed and I am up at 6 a.m. and I am on the go all day.

"Discipline leaves a lot to be desired and they lack the knowledge of drill. None of the officers seemed capable of explaining the action of the different words of command. I was longing to get out in front of the parade and explain it straightforwardly and I am sure they would have understood."

As for his task of feeding the forty-six boys,

"I think I shocked the padres when I told them I was getting some black market eggs cheap. It is very difficult to feed and cater at 3/– per head per day. It takes quite a lot of working out."

He performed his duties so capably that he was presented with an inscribed certificate.

George's faith was growing in the company of his friends from St. Paul's Church, yet his schizoid morality stayed with him. The contradiction between his professions and actions had riled Dick, but George remained impervious to all his criticism. "I do believe that God forgives if you ask his forgiveness," he claimed. God, it seemed, allowed him to be an exception. He could attend church prayer meetings, and yet swear unremittingly and soak his conversation with sex.

Each day he was reading his Bible and praying, but he chose to regard God as a device to be used rather than a Person to be loved and obeyed. God provided all that he needed, including Eva; and since this was so, he had no qualms about his relationship with her. He was aware that many of the church members disapproved of his eccentricities, though he met loving acceptance from Reg and Edith Flemming who welcomed him into their portrait studio at all hours. He introduced Eva to them and also to Joe Mullins, but when he saw that Joe was out to convert her he promptly withdrew her.

While George himself had until recently clung to a friendship with an attractive French girl, he threw a fit of rage that Eva should take a holiday with another man she had known for years. The ensuing scene was a taste of the dangers of which Dr. Hunt had warned her.

His penitence was expressed in one of his very last letters to her, for the long-standing fear of the pen was overwhelming George once more.

"I am sorry for my behaviour during the past few days—I just don't know what has happened again. I was going along o.k. and down I come. Hunt said that I wouldn't go back to that nervous state, but you must admit that I have not been normal. I was content and happy, an experience I have not had all my life.

"I doubt if there is an answer to my problem for I have mucked up my life and the mere fact that I vacillate so much tends to prove it. There are three things I can do:— (a) go back to Glasgow and see if I can mix and be happy with those I ran away from; (b) stay put and try to get on in London; (c) cut away completely and start afresh somewhere abroad. 'c' seems to be the easiest way out so I must give some thought to it.

"God has been good to me and I have the belief that everything will turn out alright—nevertheless I still worry. I suppose I will have to tell Hunt how I cried a few times this week. Somehow my slum days seem to come back to me as I write to you, Eva.

"Hoping to see you tomorrow evening."

They still met regularly, and at Christmas George took her on a fleeting visit to Glasgow where he introduced her to his sister Kathy and brother Tom. Their friendship had lasted for over a year, but by early 1953 Eva was courting her future husband. George fought against the inevitable rejection and dogged her footsteps jealously. Eventually she threatened to summon the police and broke away from him.

By May, however, the tempests were subsiding. He attributed his cure not only to his 'mate' and 'captain' Hunt, but to God. "There is nothing you can do for me," he told the psychiatrist, "that God can't do." At his final session Dr. Hunt threw out the suggestion, "Have you thought of going abroad again?" Within a few weeks he had accepted a post in Aden as Steward Supervisor for the British section of the Bechtel Wimpey Oil Corporation.

CHAPTER 7

Army for the Sultan

The George Burton who flew to Aden showed the scars of inner conflicts fought during the previous five years. Since Palestine his face had become more deeply lined and his whole figure had become more portly. Despite the prospect of Aden's rigours he looked forward to proving by the achievement of a testing job that he was still normal.

Across the bay from Aden, on the rugged promontory of Little Aden, Bechtel Wimpey were building a harbour for a refinery. Two million tons of volcanic rock were being shifted to form a breakwater, a task which employed, in addition to the oil corporation staff, fifteen hundred Arab and Somali workers. George was in charge of catering for the staff of Americans, British, Dutchmen and Italians and struggled both to keep menus varied and to ward off the ubiquitous dust. He applied himself to the gruelling work and forestalled complaints by his efficiency and cheerful humour.

After only two months an ex-Palestine Police superintendent burst upon Aden to enlist officers for a force of tribesmen being raised for the Sultan of Muscat and Oman. On being approached George pricked up his ears, for it was a 'hush-hush job', as he put it, and the pay was good.

In August 1953 he went to Khormaksar on Aden's isthmus to learn about the background of Oman. It was a fillip to him to make the acquaintance of the family of a Wing Commander and former equerry to the Queen, and he soon broke through their young daughter's shyness to become an agreeable playmate. He had bought a ciné camera, a good instrument for making himself the focal point in a group. After filming the family assiduously he quickly consented to pose for some shots of himself on horseback. In contrast to the society of the air-base town, the poverty of Aden's shanty village stirred him to vow, "If I get £3,000 I will run a home for orphans."

Early in September George boarded a boat for Muscat. His chief companion was Albert Merrell, the only other British officer, apart from the Commanding Officer, in the new Muscat and Oman Field Force. Albert was to be a major and adjutant, George captain and quartermaster. Albert, who had survived nearly four years in a Japanese prisoner of war camp, was tough, cheery and likeable.

The Sultan had given permission for a branch of the Iraq Petroleum Company to drill round Jebel Fahud, where possible oil formations had been spotted. But Jebel Fahud lay behind Oman's mountain mass, in the area controlled by the hostile Imam. And so, to afford protection for the company, it was agreed that the new force should be raised consisting of Omanis recruited, trained and commanded by British officers.

After the flat coastline of western Oman the boat slid past the mountains, black and brutal. And there, sheltering unexpectedly in a recess, was the harbour of Muscat between two sentinel forts, its buildings spotlighted and gleaming like alabaster. As the place drowsily awoke, the boat was jostled by skiffs from which glistening dark bodies dived for coins. Across the square strolled a robed figure with a black umbrella for sunshade. Muscat, the meeting-place of Indians and Arabs, presented various shades of dark skins and a variety of red, orange and white headdresses. The Omani tribesmen were lean, whiskered, flashing-eyed, most of them wearing long white shirts and cartridge belts and carrying old British army rifles. By the town walls some camels chewed superciliously, their spindly legs about to collapse under the heat.

After the polish of London George mixed easily with British officers and officials, among them the British Consul-General and the Sultan's Minister of Foreign Affairs. He was always ready to impress them with card tricks.

During his three weeks in Muscat George resorted to an American Mission Hospital where he was welcomed as a fellow-believer by Dr. Wells Thoms and his wife, and was grateful to be invited to the informal Arabic services held in their home; but he surprised them by his rigid stand against drink, flatly refusing to touch the apple juice which they offered him because they called it by its American name 'apple cider'. One of his contemporaries knew him as a 'b——— Bible puncher'.

Uncertain of the task ahead of him, George felt homesick and wrote a spate of letters to his friends in London. The replies trickled back. The Flemmings were faithful correspondents: "Dear General, We pray for you morning and evening. I know your capabilities will more than match any crisis. It's surprising how much we miss you, such is the power of personality." Another letter invited him to attend counsellors' training classes in preparation for a crusade the following spring to be led by an American evangelist, Billy Graham. Helena reported that business was slack and asked him for an allowance, but he put her letter aside.

The day's journey from Muscat to the camp of the Muscat and Oman Field Force stretched along about one hundred and fifty miles of the Batinah coast. To use the normally firm beach meant risking the loss of vehicles trapped by the tide, so George admiringly watched Albert coax and shove trucks through the stretches of soft sand on the inland route.

The camp was pitched on stony, scrubby ground near Sohar, the chief town of the Batinah. George's ciné camera captured a blissful scene of deep blue skies, bronzing sun and frothing beaches. It did not record the temperatures of 120 degrees F. aggravated by clammy winds and tormenting mosquitoes. The squat, dun tents were sometimes besieged by suffocating dust storms. But George, engaged on what he described as "the most important and most difficult job I had done in my life", met the hardships with un-flagging resilience.

As quartermaster he was for ever squeezing supplies from Sohar or Muscat. He had to negotiate with a hard and wily Indian con-tractor who could produce only the dull fare of an Indian peasant supplemented by dates and sardines from the Batinah. After being frustrated regularly by a shortage of supplies, by flour full of weevils, by tea ruined by mildew and by sugar mixed with dust, George became equally hard and wily at bargaining. Nevertheless, the food, poor though it was, became one of the Force's chief attractions to the undernourished tribesmen. As often as he could

George turned a meal into a feast, by means of a small addition to the menu, in order to boost morale. Such occasions were advertised by dancing, cheering and waving of mess-tins.

The C.O. was away much of the time searching for more officers or making plans with oil company officials. So the brunt of the recruiting and training fell upon the two Britishers assisted by two Sudanese officers and later by a few N.C.O.s. The tribespeople were truculent and at first suspicious, particularly towards non-Muslims. George's colloquial Arabic and persuasive manner were a big asset, and the food and modern rifle with which they were issued proved extra incentives. But there were many hurdles to be overcome. An arrangement might be made with a tribal chief to collect a certain number of recruits; but by the time the truck had reached the rendezvous, half of them had vanished. Many of those who did come were found to be unfit; others deserted because they were homesick or could not stand the discipline or were enticed away by the life of Sohar town.

The first recruits looked unpromising material, for discipline, hard work and hygiene were unknown to them. An assorted medley of individuals, they were in turn lethargic and boisterous, and always fickle. They insisted on bringing their families to the camp and these were scarcely prevented from joining the parades, which were anyway broken up time and again by gusts of laughter sweeping through the ranks. They found it painful to keep silence and any command might be answered with a resigned look and the expression "inshallah" (if God will). They reacted with similar resignation to their first sight of an aeroplane. "So what!" they replied, "there is nothing new under the sun." George was affectionately intrigued by them.

Ungainly though they were, they discovered a contagious enthusiasm for drill and progressed rapidly. At first it was only with reluctance that they consented to wear a khaki shirt and shorts and later red headdress, but in time that reluctance was replaced by a cocky swagger as they marched in uniform. George dressed casually in denims and a blue beret, but he knew also how to move smartly and drilled the men with patient efficiency. Swinging along with their moods he could be commanding and playful, he could laugh and be angry; and so he won their respect.

George with his father and mother
(*back left*), about 1926

Private in the Army, about 1932

Private in India, about 1936 (*front, 2nd from left*)

George Burton in charge of J.O.P. room, about 1946

George's marriage to Helena,
December 22nd, 1941

Captain George Burton, Muscat
and Oman Field Force, 1954

By the end of November some sixty men were under training and responding to discipline. The Sultan's uncle, who lived in Sohar, came over to see them and was pleased. Whereupon the C.O. took a short leave and never came back. Together with their temporary commander George and Albert proceeded with the work, but relaxed discipline and established a more communal life. They felt strongly that the Omanis should be allowed to preserve their own way of living as far as possible. Their warm understanding of the troops kept the Force from disintegrating altogether. Yet during the month's interregnum they had to face three threatened disturbances which George helped to quell by pleading and cajoling with Arab eloquence.

He loved to join in their outbursts of merriment, often organising the proceedings himself. At the end of a meal he could belch with the best of them. They expressed their affection for him by means of horseplay. He was swung aloft and carried on the upstretched arms of a score of cheering Omanis to be shoved, wrenched and prodded to their fill. He liked to see himself as 'the father of all Arabs' and persuaded Albert to take a photograph of him in Arab headdress. The pale face, double chin and fleshy nose produced a somewhat grotesque result. Fortunately Albert was tolerant both of George's conceit and of his flashes of temper, so the two men were complementary.

At the end of the year the new C.O. arrived. Lieutenant-Colonel Percy Coriat, fifty-five years old and missing an eye from service during the First World War, was an experienced soldier, upright and dedicated, who knew Arabs. He made it clear straightaway that in his view the Force was shoddy and demoralised because it lacked firm leadership and discipline. A new second-in-command had been appointed at the same time, a trim ex-trooper who shared Coriat's vision. Conflict was soon sparked off between the soldiers and the policemen. George and Albert, who in any case resented having to submit to new superiors, were told to wear proper uniform. George was required to keep a regular check on his stores and to supply lists. When they protested that the men should not be subjected to too strict discipline, they were told, "You have a distorted view of militarism." They retaliated by disregarding orders and remaining a law to themselves. Coriat also distrusted George from the start because he claimed, behind Albert's back, that he was the better officer.

In three months Coriat succeeded in raising the Force's strength to two hundred and shaping it into a reasonably organised body of men, thus shaking off a former nickname 'The Scallywag Force'. They were now ready to move to a new base from which the oil company's men could, with their equipment, blaze the trail to Jebel Fahud. The base chosen was a bay near Ras Duqqam, three hundred miles the far side of Muscat.

George was in charge of one of the parties of men. Meals had to be prepared, stores and equipment transported, the tide and quicksands negotiated and the men prevented from deserting at Muscat. From there a two days' boat trip brought the Force and oil company officials to Ras Duqqam. The sandy bay was surrounded by rocks and scrub which lent a forbidding appearance. Some hundred miles inland stretched the wastes of the Empty Quarter. Already they were being menaced by monsoon winds which would cut them off from sea communications for three months. An evaporator was erected to supply the only drinking water. Meanwhile the quartermaster was supervising the unloading of trucks and fending off scrounging local tribesmen.

During the early days the Sultan came to inspect the Force, the boat in which he was rowed to shore nearly capsizing as his enthusiastic subjects waded out to greet him. As he stepped ashore rifles were fired off spontaneously. His departure was the signal for festivities to begin. The men massed together in lines and jumped about wildly in what resembled sometimes the Highland Fling and sometimes the conga, accompanied by drums, pipes and shouting.

The monsoon was heralded by suffocating black dust. Catering was a nightmare and meals were frequently postponed. The soldiers were envious of the oil company's air-conditioned, weatherproof huts and tinned food. George and Albert fraternised with the oil men, frolicking around in matey fashion. Coriat frowned on such casual behaviour which clashed with his ideas of military conduct.

But already relationships had been irreparably damaged. Coriat stood for the authoritarian, public school type whom George, while outwardly deferential, had come to envy and detest. At the same time George could not help respecting him for his straightness and kindliness as well as his military ability. Coriat for his part tried hard to fathom George's character: so glib, cocky and hot-tempered. Why did he undermine discipline by mixing so freely with the men? And yet he was so gifted, lively and shrewd; he could be such an efficient administrator. He summed up George as a split personality.

Coriat was puzzled too by George's failure to keep lists. The man seemed to rely entirely on his own memory, which admittedly was good. Coriat scribbled a testy note, "When may I expect the list of equipment and stores?" George was touched on the raw and procrastinated. Another note followed requesting, "How much has been spent on equipment obtained from Her Majesty's Government? How much of this is for clothing? How much for arms and ammunition?" etc. George scrambled together a few rough figures which left Coriat still unsatisfied and suspicious. George felt exposed and under fire. He was blowed if he would spend hours writing at a table, keeping meticulous records as Coriat did. When a few weeks later thirteen men discovered that their rifle slings were missing from the Armoury, Coriat demanded a written explanation from the quartermaster. George bristled, assuming that he was being blamed for the loss. He anticipated the expected notice to resign by writing huffily to the Sultan's Minister of Foreign Affairs stating that after certain incidents between the C.O. and himself "it is imperative that I leave Duqqam as soon as possible".

An investigation showed that the slings had disappeared from the men's tents and not from the Armoury, and the affair was patched up; but George felt he was not trusted and hit back by spreading stories about Coriat in official circles. Years later he was troubled with guilt about his action, on hearing that already in Oman Coriat had been suffering from the early stages of a terminal illness.

Early in July 1954 Albert Merrell left "because the Force was developing more along military than police lines". One official, believing that Coriat might relinquish his command early, attempted to persuade George to wait. But Coriat stayed, and so the only solution was that George should go. He was given a testimonial to the effect that he had resigned of his own accord under the terms of his contract. The Force went on to cut a route inland for the oil company and eventually captured Nizwa, the Imam's stronghold. But no oil was discovered at Jebel Fahud.

After the strain of the previous months George considered that he was entitled to a holiday. With money in his pocket he 'lived it up' at Kuwait, Cyprus, Athens, Rome, Nice, Geneva, Zürich and Paris. He spent a day or two at each place sightseeing, picking up a girl and losing money gambling. "I was very unsettled," he recalled. "I didn't know what I was looking for. I was trying to find peace."

CHAPTER 8

The Restaurant

Three men sat talking in a dim basement room. The floor was strewn with cigarette ends and unwashed shirts, while dirty plates and tea-cups littered every other surface. In one corner stood a large table covered with papers. In another an unmade bed formed a perch for John Coe, a shy studious young man. The curate of St. Paul's, Portman Square sat beside him on a bare wooden chair, while George Burton, now the proprietor of the Regent Restaurant, Blandford Street, lay back in the only armchair. He was casually dressed in open shirt, baggy trousers and zipped pullover splashed with grease spots.

A loud bang caused the curate and John to jump up in alarm. "It's all right," George reassured them. "It's only the kids: they've dropped a thunderflash down the air vent." The curate was shaken and soon made an excuse to go. Meanwhile George told John how he had witnessed the King David Hotel in Jerusalem being blown up. Then he turned back to business.

"Now, John, it's about time you did some work for me: how can I ever get my accounts straight if you don't help me? It's been a good week for lunches, now that the taxi men have got to know me. Perhaps a miracle has even happened and I'm out of the red." John looked doubtfully at the pile of papers. Gradually, as he checked and sorted, order emerged. He had many queries. How many people had George treated to free lunches yesterday? Had he taken some money from the till to pay for those extra eggs? Was he sure he hadn't paid the butcher twice by mistake? At last John calculated that George had fallen still further behind that week, by another £10.

George had hankered after his own business since returning from Muscat. He fancied running a Bendix laundry and applied for a loan to the Canadian Sun Life Assurance Company in Glasgow. The loan was refused, but instead he was offered the chance of being trained as an insurance agent. For three weeks he studied the art of salesmanship, acquitting himself with distinction. But growing unrest gnawed his spirit. He wrote to Colin Kerr in London that he wanted to be doing Christian work.

"There's only one assurance worth selling," he preached to his trainer on the day he completed his course; "and that is John, chapter three, verse sixteen: 'God so loved the world, that He gave His only begotten Son, that whosoever believeth in Him should not perish, but have everlasting life.' " With that he jumped into his new Ford Popular and drove to London to see 'C.C.K.'

An advertisement in an evening paper caught his eye: "The Regent Restaurant, off Baker Street, takes £90 per week, v. easy hours, much scope, £1,150." George was interested, though he had only £900 behind him. On his way to discuss the project with C.C.K. he caught sight of the same advertisement in an estate agent's window. "Too much of a coincidence," he commented, and C.C.K. agreed. Had not George only just received training in salesmanship and experience in catering? Could not the restaurant become a sort of mission hall within the parish of St. Paul's? Together they prayed that if it were His will God would produce the necessary money. C.C.K. introduced him to Charles West, a member of his congregation who was a solicitor, and he set in motion the legal processes towards its purchase.

'Restaurant' was a pretentious description of the place. It had been established in 1870 and since then the décor had hardly been disturbed. The mahogany pew seats and brown and cream paint-work achieved the effect of a dingy railway compartment. Its small size made the ground floor dining-room homely but uneconomic; it could accommodate a mere thirty-eight people. From the kitchen the meals were sent up on a lift.

As negotiations proceeded, various difficulties became apparent. Above the restaurant were several floors of flats whose tenants were looked after by the landlord's manageress, Mrs. Levy, and George would be required to serve them some twenty breakfasts a week. The lease had only three years to run and he would be expected to re-decorate the premises that year. On checking the inventory he claimed that some of the articles listed were either broken or missing.

But George, inclined to optimism, rose early to visit Covent Garden and Smithfield Market. The appeal of proprietorship, and especially of being able to serve the Lord, enabled him to view the mountains as molehills. The Lord would surely provide. And He did provide by prompting two Christian friends each to loan George £250, while his bank permitted an overdraft of £500. On March 25th, 1955 George Burton assumed ownership of the restaurant. Colin Kerr came to launch the venture with prayer and various St. Paul's friends rallied to his aid.

George had met John Coe at a church service. The lanky accounts clerk responded to the interest of the older man. George even offered to teach him to drive and generously loaned him his car. In return John undertook to tackle the finances and submit the income tax returns. His task was complicated by George's unbusinesslike methods; he undercharged for meals and lost the luncheon vouchers. To John's considerable relief, however, the authorities acknowledged that the restaurant was running at a loss and claimed no tax.

After church on Sunday evenings, and several nights a week too, a group of John's friends, Jay, Cynthia and others, would set to work like a band of slaves, scrubbing floors, polishing tables and peeling mountains of potatoes. Sometimes they finished with a supper of George's favourite meal, 'eggy bacon'. Always they combined in prayer entreating God to deliver George from debt. Their faith sustained him through his trials and he depended on their companionship at weekends when he stayed in their homes or went with them on car outings. Often they visited their disabled friend Peter.

Roland, George's earliest link with St. Paul's, was an electrician, and so he fitted a system of lights for contacting the kitchen direct from the dining-room. He was a friend and George's partner in prayer through various crises.

A Mr. Stephenson volunteered to wash the outside paintwork. A broken ladder rung caused 'Steve' to fall, breaking his arm, and George's insurance did not cover his helper. As if in retribution, on the very next day George badly bruised his right index finger in a door.

A gloomy letter reached Charles West. "Things are not too good and I am in the 'red' at the end of the first two weeks, and will be even more so at the end of the third. I am learning the hard way." He went on to describe his plan to open the restaurant in the evenings on a 'fifty-fifty' basis with a couple he had met. But the lease forbade this and George was baulked in his intentions.

His dominant difficulty was his relationship with Mrs. Levy. Poor Charles received a stream of complaints about George from her solicitors, many of them justified, some trivial. The chief contention concerned the provision of breakfast for the upstairs tenants. This invariably caused a slanging match, sometimes on the street, between George and Mrs. Levy. He found her a doughty opponent and for once had to admit defeat. "I am afraid," he confessed to Charles, "that there is no one (human) who could cope with her. She pulls out every one of the tricks, including the feminine ones." He tried hard to co-operate with her and for most of the time the conflict simmered, exploding in occasional bursts. One skirmish led George to protest to Charles, "It is impossible for anyone to be as tolerant as I have been. Am I allowed peace and quiet? Why should she shout at me that she will see my lease is not renewed? She is a horribly rude woman and is doing her best to make things awkward for me."

For economy's sake George took to sleeping in the basement. This was forbidden by the terms of his lease, and it taxed Charles' ingenuity to defend his client. This infringement, however, meant that George was at hand to deal with a series of plumbing calamities. One morning he was woken by the sound of rain, which proved to be an overflow from the main water tank. George persuaded the plumber to do a temporary repair, but Mrs. Levy was reluctant to let it have any further attention. The walls and woodwork were damaged, beside the loss of a morning's trade. A few days later, just as the customers were arriving at mid-day, the water overflowed again. For four hours it flooded down the stairs and the plumber would not come until George paid his previous bill. "I was nearly at the end of my tether but faith kept me going," he reported to Charles. "Seemingly the pipes are blocked and whenever it rains it is like the monsoon in India in my backyard. Thank God I am not responsible for structural repairs."

George had resilience to combat these troubles, and there were some encouragements. One day there was a queue of four people waiting for seats. But what cheered him most were the opportunities to put his new 'Operation Faith' into action. A Scotsman wanted to switch his order of rolls from a neighbouring café to George, but George out of loyalty to his neighbour declined. An hour later he received a fresh order to supply sixteen coffees a day and recognised this as a token of God's approval. When his chef told him she was leaving, George prayed with Roland, and the next day she changed her mind. Another result of Operation Faith was he smoked only twenty cigarettes in ten days. After George began to speak openly about Christ, he could soon boast that some of his patrons were saying grace before meals. The Child Adoption Centre next door brought a sorry trickle of customers to whom he often read the Bible story of the woman taken in adultery.

His growing acquaintance with the Christian faith made George guilty about his treatment of Helena. For four years they had hardly seen each other, one exception being a remarkable glimpse he caught of her just before taking on the restaurant. To help meet the cost of the business his bank manager was pressing him to sell the car. C.C.K. and Charles, however, were encouraging him to follow his inclination to keep it for Christian work. The issue became a spiritual conflict and in his distraction George went for a night's bridge. Next morning, conscious that he was disobeying God, he drove out to sell the car.

As he hunted for a garage in Kensington he noticed a familiar figure walking down some steps—Helena! But he did not dare face her. Instinctively he turned the car round and accelerated frenziedly across a major road. An oncoming lorry swept his car on to its side. "He must be dead," George heard someone say as they forced the door open, enabling him to struggle out. There was Helena at the corner, but she walked away without recognising him. Then in wonder at God's intervention he exclaimed, "Yes, God, You were right; now I can't sell my car."

Recollection of the incident haunted him. Was God directing him to be reconciled with Helena? He was surprised to receive via his bank a letter from her solicitors informing him that she wished to institute 'proceedings for dissolution of her marriage'. He did not know where she was living. But early one June evening God seemed to be telling him to see Helena. He was learning that God requires instant obedience, so without washing or changing he clambered into his car.

Just before the crash he had seen her coming from a door in Courtfield Gardens, so he drove there and sat in the car praying that God would bring her to him. For nearly three hours he prayed and watched and waited. As he said the Lord's Prayer for the hundredth time, there before his eyes was Helena walking past the car, trim and dainty as ever. He sweated and sat paralysed. His impulse was to drive away and escape. Yet God had sent him there and brought her to him. "Lord, help me," he whispered as he walked after her. "Helena," he called softly. She swung round and stood rooted like a startled rabbit, her surprise intensified by the half light. "God has sent me to you," he tried to calm her. She hesitated, for she was confronted by a large grease-stained man, not the slim immaculate George she had first known. His altered appearance had blinded her from recognising him at the car accident. Eventually she agreed to see him the following week.

Then it was George's turn to be afraid again. He felt sure that she had set detectives after him and he would be arrested. They had tea and both survived. After that they arranged to meet every Thursday. George found that her walk at nine p.m. on that June evening was not her normal routine but had been decided upon on the spur of the moment. Gradually ideas of divorce faded, though reconcilation was still remote.

At the restaurant George continued to be pitched from brief moments of elation to long lonely hours of surging despair. Without his Christian friends he would have been sunk. He clung to Charles West, consulting him about everything, until Charles dreaded the entanglement of the daily phone call.

George had confided his fear of writing to C.C.K. who assured him that "nothing is impossible if you believe". Accordingly he bravely seized his pen and unburdened himself to Charles in long disjointed letters.

"With my antipathy to letter writing I don't know how I am able to pick up this pen to write to you. There is no money in this place, I don't want money for myself and I would willingly run this place with a couple of Christian people and give all to Christian work. If it was God's will that I took over this restaurant then He will find an answer. 'Faith'; I have it now, and yet I contradict myself by saying I am a little worried. The past few days I have been a bit depressed, but FAITH has kept me going."

This brave, pathetic faith stopped him giving way to unrelieved hopelessness. At the same time he steeled himself to abide by principles of honesty and straightness; he was scrupulous, for instance, about paying his debts. He often resisted the temptation to seek female company by depositing his day's takings with a friend who lived nearby. But sometimes the pull was too strong and when he yielded his slowly awakening conscience was troubled.

"C.C.K. has managed to get me to accept that I am a Christian and now I openly say I am one, yet I still do things that I am ashamed of. I had a night out last night, dancing and taking one of the opposite sex home. Have I sinned? I didn't go to the extreme but I know the thoughts and actions were sin. I am sorry I let Him down and I am sure He will forgive."

Meanwhile the dampness was causing the bricks to crumble and the stairs to rot, and was damaging electric light fittings. Water dripped on to the cooking stove and the dining-room seats, and when George complained he was reminded that the interior was his responsibility and that the only decoration he had carried out was to paint the staircase "in a somewhat rough manner". On top of this he was beset by staff troubles. The couple he had employed with such high hopes proved unreliable. They came each morning with large shopping bags which George later believed they filled with his stores of food to take home. Debts mounted and his bank manager refused to grant him another overdraft.

His confidence was waning, as he told Charles.

"I am BROWNED OFF. One should not be fed up if they have their Lord really encased inside—so perhaps I haven't enough of Him, although I am willing to serve Him to the best of the ability that He has given me. I realise I am letting my few friends down as they had such faith in me; but I have lost faith in my ability to be a business man. He put me here and I feel He is taking me out. If nothing else I have worked for a few months and come to know my Lord better. For years I have been boastful in my own way — not in His name."

Then God sent an angel to his rescue: a short, stout Italian-born Cockney known as Madame Louise Tullio. She was a homely figure with brown eyes twinkling from a face which showed the lines of a hard life. She arrived at the restaurant declaring that she had come from the Labour Exchange and was going to work for George. "I have been in the catering business all my life and I can get double the money you are offering me, but I only want a job for a few months. I am going to help you out, but as soon as your business is on its feet you will have to get out because I shall be leaving." Having employed herself she paddled off, promising she would start on Monday morning.

From then on the Regent Restaurant was revolutionised, its proprietor turning to clay in her hands. "Sack the woman you employ to work the lift," she ordered; "I can do it quicker myself." At dinner time the meals shot up from the kitchen faster than ever before. Next she swayed George to sack the dishonest couple and in their place she brought her friend, Mitzi, to be waitress. She made him buy food in bulk and taught him how to peel potatoes more economically. She spotted that he was not only being cheated by tradesmen but also sucked by some of his customers who were taking advantage of his generous nature. She propounded to him her father's dictum, "If you've got tuppence, save a penny for to-morrow"; but that went against George's grain. More than once she came upon him crying about his business worries. "What's the matter, Mr. Burt?" she inquired tenderly, and consoled him with a recitation of her sumptuous menu. She filled the part of the kind, motherly woman whom he constantly needed.

Under Madame Tullio's genius the reputation of the Regent Restaurant soared. Her shepherd's pie was the most popular dish of all, enhanced by herbs and golden-brown onions. Steam puddings left over from one day became a tasty 'Baroness Pudding' decked with jam the next. Taxi drivers queued for her meals, shouting down the hatch, "Auntie, don't forget my apple tart." George's laughter echoed through the informal dining-room. He was the gay host, untidy but cordial, and diplomatic enough to conciliate a customer over whom he spilt a plate of rice pudding.

Within a month Madame Tullio summoned George to the kitchen. Opening an envelope she took out fifty pound notes. "I am lending you this money, Mr. Burt," she explained. "Now take it to the butcher to pay your bill. Show him this list of prices and tell him this is all you are prepared to pay for your meat. And if he doesn't agree, you're going elsewhere." To George's amazement the butcher capitulated.

By June 1956 the business was on an even footing. "Now sell and get out," she ordered. "If you don't you will be back where you were before I came." Obediently George sold. With debts discharged he was left with £16 and his Ford Popular; in his own words, "broke financially, but built spiritually". He borrowed a camp bed at John Coe's digs where he stayed for some weeks, and then resorted to Ireland. By the autumn he was itching to travel again.

CHAPTER 9

Cyprus

It was hard to escape from 'K' Camp. The ugly settlement rose from a treeless waste of ruddy soil ten miles from Nicosia. The huts of the 500 Greek detainees were separated into compounds, presenting a network of cages linked by catwalks. The whole camp was enclosed by a double perimeter of barbed wire fifteen feet high. At night the blaze of searchlights revealed killer dogs straining at the leash as they patrolled the walks.

An atmosphere of tension surrounded the Superintendent, Adrian Arnold, and his fifty warders. Their charges included genuine Eoka terrorists, but many were mere schoolboy suspects rounded up after British civilians had been shot in the streets of Nicosia. In common with other Greek Cypriots and in token of their resentment of British colonial rule they were supporters of the Enosis movement for union with Greece.

George had not studied the political situation. In his financial straits he had been attracted to the job of sergeant warder by the salary of £1,000, for which he had signed a years' contract from November 1956. He saw the detainees not as bloodthirsty brigands but as people who laughed and cried and quarrelled, people with homes and families, but with nothing else to do now except play football and marbles and make things in fretwork. At least one had also worked in a London restaurant. Like the Superintendent, he interpreted the riotous bonfire of camp furniture which followed Archbishop Makarios' release from the Seychelles in January 1957 as a spontaneous gesture of joy, not hatred.

George was heartily disliked by most of his fellow warders, some of whom were ex-army or navy officers, some policemen. Almost all were hard-drinking and hard-swearing. They could not trust George; he would not be a party to any fiddle and a warder who showed interest in the prisoners was an obvious security risk. Many resented his tendency to pry into others' affairs. When one of them fell in love with the daughter of the Greek Cypriot manager of a leading hotel, his colleagues warned him of the dangers of this association, but George was alone in encouraging the match. He made a few friends, but none of them really came to know him.

In the mess while others drank George sipped Coca-Cola. They could not understand such a queer fish. On his first night in 'K' Camp George's room-mate was aghast to see him kneel at his bed-side and applied next morning to change his room, to avoid sharing with a 'Bible puncher'. The news soon spread through the camp that Burton was religious. Their aloofness and sneers, real and imagined, thrust him into his shell and he fancied that he was the hated topic of every conversation. He emerged to encourage one or two to attend a camp service, but the others were either on duty, sleeping, or out of camp.

George recalled bitterly how he had learnt at St. Paul's that it was the Christian's lot to suffer persecution. In contrast to the cosiness of St. Paul's, where Christians had listened and understood, he was despised, hated, ostracised. If only C.C.K. were there to advise him. He retired to the only place of privacy, the toilet, and opened his Bible. He was too agitated to read and could only pray tearfully, "I do want to serve You, Lord, and tell them about You, but they won't listen to me."

He pined for a letter from his Christian friends, but despite their promises after three weeks he had heard only from faithful Jay, John and crippled Minnie. The whole of one night George stayed up scribbling letters to them all: C.C.K., Reg and Edith, John and Jay, Cynthia, Minnie, Frank, Peter and Kathleen. He described how unhappy he was, how he was missing them, how the job seemed to be a 'wash out'. Soon a sheaf of letters came back. "My dear old friend," wrote C.C.K., "The trouble with you, George, is that you are much too subjective . . . At the restaurant you were blessed, but your spiritual life rested on the close friendships that you had then. You have to discover the secret of rejoicing in Christ in loneliness and perplexity . . ." George had left his car with C.C.K., who promised to sell it for him. But a faulty battery caused the elderly Vicar some awkward moments and he was glad to procure a buyer.

Joe Mullins was praying that George would have constant victory over temptation; Cynthia, John and Jay wrote chattily about their romances; Minnie was praying for him each day and hoping that he was reading his daily Scripture Union portion. George was comforted to know that someone wanted him and he hoarded each letter.

Christmas only exaggerated his misery. He went to the Anglican church in Nicosia where both service and congregation were too formal for his liking; but he introduced himself to the Archdeacon who invited him to a musical evening at his home. George felt out of place until he discovered a crippled boy who was staying there; in that child he saw himself, the odd one out. George attended further evenings at the Archdeacon's home, but was looking for "deeper Christian fellowship". The Archdeacon for his part felt uneasy with George and was perplexed by the gulf between his assertions and his behaviour. One evening an unobtrusive young man asked, "Are you George Burton?" "Yes." "Oh, we've been looking for you. The Reverend Colin Kerr wrote to say that you were in Cyprus."

Next day over a cup of tea Stephen Popper explained that he belonged to a group of evangelical Christians who would welcome George at their Gospel services and Bible Studies. George was overjoyed and saw the invitation as an answer to prayer. The little group, mostly Christian Brethren, met even for the Sunday service in the cosy informality of each other's homes. As he listened to intricate verses being unravelled, George's soul was nourished.

He was impressed that such a variety of people could be deeply united in Christ. There were British, Cypriots and Americans, Army and R.A.F. officers and other ranks, regulars and national servicemen. One of the latter was Julian, a tall gauche youth with a shock of red hair to whom George attached himself, and they arranged to meet in off-duty hours. Julian, in turn, welcomed George's paternal friendship and prayed diligently for him.

George was summing up these Christians. On the pro side were their transparent sincerity and devotion to God, their personal intimate knowledge of Jesus Christ, their reverence for the Bible, their insistence on conversion, their kindly concern for people, and their hospitality. On the con side were their narrow cliquishness and use of jargon, their rigid conventions, and their quaint piety which formed a cover for the same petty jealousies and conceits as any group of people harbour. If you adopted their ways in language, dress and behaviour they accepted you; otherwise they looked askance or tried to squeeze you into their mould.

Many of them doubted whether George were a properly converted Christian. How could he smoke and still be a Christian? And was he not rather familiar with the ladies? Why, he actually danced with Stephen's sister. They would have been outraged had they learnt that he was married, a fact which George carefully concealed. So they kept George on the fringe of the group, and did not introduce him to the 'inner circle' meeting, the Breaking of Bread on Sunday mornings.

George was hurt and stored up his ammunition against them. They seemed intent more on maintaining the glow of their own little fellowship than spreading it to others. If Christ meant so much to them, why did they clutch Him to themselves? At one prayer meeting he exposed their insularity with scathing criticism of a beach party they were organising: they were excluding others so that they could enjoy the company of their own boy and girl friends. Joe Mullins had just written to him, "May the Lord give you *souls*, George." "Which one of you," he burst out, "has ever led a soul to Christ?" Then he remembered that he himself had never won a soul and turned the thought into a silent prayer for a recent addition to the group, a girl called Joy Smith.

Despite such blasts George returned to 'K' Camp strengthened by the comradeship of the Christians. Within the camp his sufferings persisted, until a remarkable incident took place. One midnight he was patrolling the inner catwalks surrounding the huts. Turning a corner he saw a dog thirty yards ahead. It had shaken free of its handler and was moving towards him. This Dante was trained to kill on sight and he had a particularly vicious reputation, having killed three times and savaged two handlers. George froze with terror, and prayed. Miraculously Dante stopped motionless in his tracks. Inch by inch George sidled up to the wire, then scrambled over to safety.

'K' Camp was soon buzzing with the story. Men who had previously ignored George now approached him and even the toughest asked him questions about God, prayer and the Bible. He found

6

himself directing them towards Jesus Christ and their need of a personal faith in Him. He became at least respected, if not exactly liked, and was voted on to the social committee. Every month there was an Open Evening to which ladies could be invited. George was in his element teaching some of the men to dance to the tune 'Bo-weevil'. But during his off-duty hours he was not content to stay in the mess drinking and playing cards or darts. He preferred to be independent, and so he bought a car. With it he gave lifts to the Christians, especially the young ladies, to and from their meetings. He also enjoyed taking them sightseeing at Kyrenia and its romantic old castle of St. Hilarion. Sometimes he went for a drive with the Superintendent. Few would have suspected that at other times his car carried him to the infamous Tanzimat Street in Nicosia where he sought relief for his restlessness and loneliness.

In the summer of 1957 a temporary truce made movement in the island easier. None the less George took unwarranted risks and, contrary to regulations, went about alone and unarmed, even down Nicosia's 'Murder Mile'. He delivered messages, sweets and toys to the homes of detainees, until a colleague was shot on a similar mission.

He found an outlet for his love of children at the Deaf and Dumb School, and later at the Blind School where Mrs. Greenland welcomed his visits; for her young charges clearly loved 'Uncle George' who played with their rattling football and drove them to the beach. He made himself useful by inducing others to hang pictures, reorganise the library and construct a concrete path. Out of those who helped at the school George was the only one to be presented with a book, and several of the children wrote to him afterwards.

Helena was now writing to acknowledge the allowance which he was sending to her regularly; by the end of the year she was signing herself, 'your loving wife'. With the Flemmings she attended St. Paul's several times and C.C.K. grew optimistic. He foresaw George and Helena going into business together and using their home as a meeting-place for Christians. Writing from India Joe Mullins had the vision of George becoming the warden of a boarding school for Anglo-Indians with Helena as housemother. "Is Helena saved yet?" he inquired.

George himself was eager to serve the Lord, but association with the Brethren had laid bare his own ignorance of the Christian faith.

Not understanding their Bible-steeped language he was unable to enter fully into their discussions. Someone suggested that he should tackle the Emmaus Bible School correspondence course which required reading the Bible without having to write lengthy answers. Enlisting the aid of Stephen Popper and others for the difficult questions he embarked on the course.

In July he withdrew for two weeks' leave to a small flat overlooking beautiful Kyrenia where he resolved to pursue his studies. But he hated being on his own and could not concentrate. He needed company, and as he got to grips with the course persuaded Christian friends to join him. It was exciting for George to appropriate facts which he had only groped after at St. Paul's. He learnt that through his conversion at the Elgin Place Mission he had been born again into God's family. A child of God cannot be 'unborn' or ever snatched out of God's hands. The story of Nicodemus in the third chapter of St. John's Gospel became George's favourite, and his sole criterion of a Christian was 'Are you born again?'

Recently he had called himself 'Evangelical C. of E.', but the Emmaus course made him question some of the cherished traditions of the Anglican Church. What was the point of infant baptism? Why should there be bishops and what biblical authority had they? Why indeed should there be clergy at all, claiming that they were the spiritual élite? To George it was common-sense that each member of the church ought to be a missionary, and that new converts should be trained for evangelism and leadership.

Asked to write out his personal testimony of conversion, he declined with the words,

> "In my first letter I mentioned that I was not prepared to go into my past and present history. I know that I have been born again. It is a personal thing between my Lord and myself."

He was relieved to know that all his sins past, present and future were forgiven through the shedding of Christ's blood, but his own chronically sinful ways still bothered him. It was not only that he did things which shocked other Christians; they were peripheral to his angry, jealous, deceitful thoughts and words. In George's view a Christian might sin more on a picnic than at a dance.

When he came to consider the behaviour which was fitting to a

Christian, his conscience was alarmed and he staved off any probing. Faced with a question about which activities a Christian should avoid, he gave an evasive answer:

> "Obviously you want me to mark cinema, dancing, smoking and card playing. My belief is that it is a question of degree. If one does something to excess and neglects the work of the Lord because of it, it naturally becomes sinful—even physical exercise, although one should keep the body healthy."

Nevertheless, he intended go give up smoking and asked Julian to pray that God would help him. He recognised that his life could not hold a candle to the example of other Christians; but in one aspect he determined to surpass them. "Lord, let me win souls," he prayed. His friendship with young Joy Smith was growing and he longed to lead her to Christ. He became a regular guest at her home and made a point of getting to know her parents, who soon came to accept her unusual friend. He drove her around the island and even taught her to dance at a club, at the same time talking about Christianity.

One day, while praying, he sensed that God was moving him to go and speak to Joy. He called at her home and was invited to a meal, after which he agreed to drive Joy's parents to the army mess. His opportunity had apparently gone; but as they reached the mess Mrs. Smith remembered something and asked, "George, would you mind popping back and telling Joy?" He was soon back helping her wash the dishes. Then he braced himself to say, "Joy, will you fetch a Bible? I want to show you something." They sat down and he went on, "Have you ever said a prayer to Jesus and asked Him to come into your life?" No, but she was ready to. George explained from the Bible that Jesus Christ was knocking at the door of her life, and then he encouraged her to say a prayer inviting Him to enter. She did so gladly, and George wrote agog to tell C.C.K. and Joe Mullins that he had won his first soul. Subsequently he kept in touch with Joy who went on to train at a Bible College.

August was stifling hot and George was relieved to escape to the cooler air of the Troodos mountains for the annual Christian conference. With the Bible course behind him he felt more confident in the company of other Christians.

Near the expiry of his contract he was offered a year's extension. He hesitated and thought and prayed, for he was bent now upon discovering God's will for every step. He was eager to serve Him, but should he stay to serve Him in Cyprus or should he return to England? His prayer was interrupted by a knock at the door and a letter from John Coe's fiancée, Jay: "Remembering how well you get on with children, I wonder if you have heard of this new venture of the Rev. David Sheppard at the Dockland Settlement in the East End of London?" Who was the Rev. David Sheppard? It did not matter. Surely this was God's wonderful guidance, and George wrote back, "Yes, I believe God is calling me to work with the Rev. David Sheppard." He prayed with Stephen and others about this new step, and there he left it. He decided to return forthwith to London, and November saw him flying out of Cyprus, his 'gash' job completed.

CHAPTER 10

On the Mount

On arrival in London George made no inquiries about David Sheppard. If God purposed to link him with Sheppard, then let God bring it about. Meanwhile he dismissed the idea from his mind. Instead he resumed connection with his friends from St. Paul's and, since he felt stranded without one, searched for a car. His sentimental attachment to his former 'NGG 169' led him to track down its current owners. When they confided to him that they had just considered buying another car, George coaxed them into selling the Ford Popular back to him. "More than a coincidence" was how he interpreted the transaction.

Hearing that his sister Kathy was in hospital he set out for Glasgow. He drove through the foggy night to reach Scotland by dawn, nodding at the wheel. His car slewed into the verge and somersaulted. George was pulled out, apparently unhurt, and someone handed him a cigarette. "No thank you," he replied, "I gave up smoking yesterday." After having his broken rib strapped in a hospital, he insisted on driving the badly damaged car into Glasgow that same afternoon, to sleep for twenty-four hours.

Then he went to see Kathy and lost no time in switching his new missionary zeal on to her, asking if she had ever been converted. "Is this all you have come from London for?" she exploded, and nurses came to escort him away. A little later, however, he succeeded in reconciling her and stayed in her home for a few weeks. He proved that, even with money in his pocket, he could resist the lure of Glasgow's night life and the pull of bridge. Mostly he stayed indoors reading Christian literature and writing to friends about his car crash. During a prayer meeting at the Faith Mission he resolved to make a donation of two pounds to the Mission. Someone then prayed that God would furnish two pounds for some urgent need, and George's faith was strengthened.

He also attended the church of St. George's, Tron, where he was gripped by the gospel preaching of the Rev. Tom Allan. One Sunday night George returned so late that Kathy and her husband Willy were already in bed. As George knelt over his bed, Willy nudged Kathy: "He must have a sore stomach." "No, he's praying," she whispered. Half an hour later George was still in the same position. "Not still praying, is he?" muttered Willy. "He must have sinned more than usual today." Next morning when Kathy told her brother to keep better hours he explained, "There were one or two souls I was trying to seek."

He was unsure about his future, but with a deepening sense of God's control he left Glasgow and took a quiet room in North London, where he stayed for three months. He celebrated Christmas there over a Hungarian-style meal with Helena and her youngest sister. Later he referred to this period as his time 'on the mount', because he experienced a special intimacy with God. Not only did he speak to God, but God seemed to speak to him. The Holy Spirit became a real person, and so did the Devil. "I spend the majority of my time," he wrote to Colin Kerr, "alone in my room with my Lord, studying His word, talking things over with Him and thanking Him for His patience with me."

From childhood he had yearned to be a missionary, and now he felt ready to realise that ambition. He visualised himself in charge of a little mission hall and running a shop as his base for directing people to the hall. He applied to the London City Mission which he had been afraid of approaching in the days when he worked across the road for Godfrey Davis. He was informed that he was too old to be considered for training, but it was suggested that he might think about ordination. "I am not too old," George fumed afterwards. "If the Lord wants me in the L.C.M., He will fit me in there." But he concluded a little later, "I don't feel called to any particular organisation."

It suited him better to be a freelance evangelist. Some days he would descend from 'the mount' to enter a library and place himself next to someone reading *The Times*. Pointing to the Bible text on the front page he would observe, "Isn't it fitting?" and a conversation about Christianity often ensued. He turned his car into a 'mission box' offering lifts to people standing at bus stops. On being thanked, he threw off the remark, "That's all right, the car doesn't belong to me," adding after a pause, "it belongs to the Lord." Sometimes he placed a Bible on the seat so that his passenger had to pick it up. Then he inquired, "I wonder when you last held a Bible in your hand?"

George seemed to be on a hot line to God. One evening as he was praying in his room, he sensed that God was calling him to help Minnie, his crippled friend. Straightaway he drove to her through thick snow and was just in time to rescue her after she had fallen and hurt herself.

"I know now that I am a missionary," he told Colin Kerr. He wondered whether God was stirring him, with his knowledge of Arabic, to return to the Arab world as a Christian worker. Then Helena suggested the possibility of their setting up a business partnership with her sister Mariska in Brazil. But the scheme was fruitless. George stipulated that before they could work together from a home Helena would have to experience convertion. Once or twice she accompanied him to a St. Paul's service, but she was a long way from sharing his views. A friend dared to point out to George that they were utterly incompatible and could never live together unless he were to drop his overbearing manner towards her. Infuriated though he was by such a stab of truth, he was beginning to consider divorce. But one morning, as he lay in bed praying, he was moved to look at his Bible. It fell open at verse eleven of I Corinthians, chapter seven: 'let not the husband put away his wife'. That was God's command to him, and he clung to it. They settled for the routine of seeing each other one day a week.

George's dilatory attitude towards finding a job veiled his impatience to start the special work which he believed God had for him. Then out of the blue came an invivitation to visit the Dockland No. 1 Settlement, as it then was, in East London's Canning Town. It came from the chaplain, the Rev. David Gardner, to whom George's name had been given as a possible youth leader for the new work there. Gardner was impressed with George, as he wrote to David Sheppard: "He has had a deep experience of conversion, yet, having knocked about the world, has not lost touch with his own kind. He has administrative and organising ability." He added a caution, "You would need to inquire into his domestic affairs."

One morning his landlady handed George an envelope. Tearing it open he read the letter for which he had been waiting. It was signed by David Sheppard and ran:

> "We have not been able to meet yet, but our Chaplain has told me about you. Since we have started our clubs in the last few days we have come to feel that our present staff is going to find it difficult to cope properly. I wonder whether it is at all conceivable that you might be free to think of coming to us as a whole time club leader."

George lost no time. Within two days he was face to face with the imposing figure of the handsome Rev. David Sheppard, former cricket captain of Sussex and England. Since leaving Cambridge, Sheppard had been ordained into the Anglican ministry and had served for the past two years as curate in a North London parish. There he had grappled with some of the Church's problems in a city area and seen the need to train Christians for youth work. It was this that had led him to accept the post as Warden of the new Mayflower Family Centre, as the Settlement was now called.

George greeted Sheppard by throwing down the challenge, "I don't play cricket. I don't like cricket. I don't know anything about cricket." "We won't fall out over that," returned Sheppard and spent the next few hours with him. "If I come here," George warned him, "you'll find out sooner or later, so I might as well tell you now, I've cheated, gambled and lied for most of my life. I haven't got on with my wife and we're legally separated now." But there were limits to his candour, and neither then nor at any other time did he disclose to Sheppard the existence of a son. If the matter troubled his conscience at all he could stifle it by working for the good of other young people. "But, I know," he went on, "that the Lord Jesus Christ has blotted out the past. I believe He has given me the power to lead a better life and I want to serve Him and lead souls to Him. I have always wanted to work among young people and I believe I could work with you." David Sheppard thought so too. Here was no new convert: through the painful years of rehabilitation he had proved God's power, and other Christians were ready to vouch for his unusual gift with young people.

David Sheppard explained that some months previously the Mayflower Family Centre's Council had taken over the premises of the Dockland Settlement, which had carried on social work there for fifty years. The new Centre was interdenominational but held Church of England services in its chapel. In such a densely populated area as Canning Town there was no question of poaching members of other churches. Sheppard saw the priority now to be not so much to run clubs for the East Enders as to train them to run their own, a task that would take many years to accomplish. After being closed since the previous summer the clubs had been re-opened, even though there was no senior youth leader.

"Would you like to come and see the teenage club?" asked Sheppard. The two men walked across the open courtyard. George had already taken off his new overcoat, Homburg hat and white kid gloves, and as they approached the club he hesitated for a moment, compelling the Warden to stop with him. Undoing his top shirt button he whipped off his tie and stuffed it into his pocket. From then on he was seldom seen to wear one.

At the club rooms he took in the situation at a glance. Some thirty teenagers were in the main room which was furnished with a table tennis table, a darts board, a canteen counter and various easy chairs and small tables. A billiards table filled the other room and occupied a handful of boys. There was no record player or background music.

A short harassed-looking young lady noticed the visitor's arrival and Sheppard introduced George to her. "This is Jean Lodge Patch, our girls' club leader," he said, and left George with her. Jean had been a medical social worker, and although her sociology degree gave her recognition as a youth leader she lacked experience of club work. Details such as whether to charge a deposit on billiard balls and cues seemed weighty matters to her. She had heard of George's visit and welcomed him with relief and interest. His air of solid competence and complete ease of manner with the young people spread a sense of security. "Would you keep an eye on the boys in the billiards room?" she asked him. "What an ignorant female," he thought, but he decided he could work with her and obliged. Her own first impressions were noted in her diary that night. "He had remarkable control of the boys and knew their names within a few minutes. He knows the game well, and soon four of them were playing so seriously that they forgot their cigarettes and were concentrating on the table."

During the next week George paid several calls to the Mayflower and the club. A helper was officiously collecting subscriptions from the boys as they arrived. 'No subs, no admission' was the rule, and the helper intended to enforce it. Such an attitude did not make sense to George. Surely the boy was more important than the shilling?

At the weekly service he was invited to say something about himself. Looking round him he caught the eye of each boy and girl in turn. Having gained their attention, he told them of his life as a teenager in Glasgow and how he had come to trust in the Lord Jesus Christ. "I've done many wrong things since then," he admitted, "but one thing I know. The Lord Jesus lives right here," thumping his chest, "and He can live in your hearts too." Without labouring the point, he deliberately switched off to tell them how he taught soldiers to drill in Oman when they did not know the difference between left and right. "I'll tell you what we did," he said with the air of a magician about to disclose a mystery. "We made them each carry a small stone in their right hand, and we said, 'Turn to the stone', when we wanted them to turn right." By now the teenagers were interested. If this was a club service they did not mind listening.

"I've told you enough about myself: now what about you?" George turned to them. And within minutes he had them all telling him what they did. A third were still at school, but of the others the majority described their occupation as 'self-employed' or, more honestly, 'fiddling'. One boy, who journeyed to Covent Garden each morning for his uncle's fruit stall, found that the strange new man was familiar with the market too.

Jean was soon convinced that George was the man for the job, and never at any time in the next eight years did she waver from that conviction. Not all of the Mayflower Council were quite so sure. After all, what experience of youth work had he, and what formal qualifications could he show? Besides, his blunt manner offended some of them. "He has such odd, staring eyes," one man observed as he sought to define the impression of mental instability which shot out at moments from this burly and disturbing character. His separation from his wife raised another uncertainty. George indicated, however, that he intended to see Helena from time to time and wanted to invite her to stay with him for occasional nights at the Centre.

If the discussion had taken place a few months earlier, the Council might have reached a different decision; but the clubs were already open, and the need for a man of George's calibre was patent. He seemed transparently honest about his weaknesses, and his sincere desire to serve God satisfied David Sheppard and several others that it was worth taking the risk of having him. George was invited to the Centre for a trial period. "If he's impossible we can ask him to leave," was the theory. George, sensitive as always to others' opinions about him realised that the Council was by no means unanimously in favour of engaging him. "If the Lord wants me to stay I shall stay," came his characteristic response.

David Sheppard had asked George to attend a conference of Christian youth leaders which was being held over the Easter weekend of 1958. The main speaker was the distinguished Sir Basil Henriques and George was quite unable to conceal his amazement that a Christian gathering should look to a prominent Jew for advice on running their youth clubs. The concept that there was a body of knowledge common to all youth work was one that he could not yet grasp. To him a Christian youth club was one where the leader was aiming above all to introduce his members to a real faith in the Lord Jesus Christ. The club programme was of secondary importance. The issue was so clear to him that he always maintained that a child of ten who knew Christ could run a Christian youth club better than the most highly qualified youth leader who did not know Him personally. However, he agreed with every word of David Sheppard's address and was on tenterhooks to start the job to which God had called him.

After the conference he told his landlady, "I'll be leaving at the end of the week," and that night she heard a lusty voice singing, 'He leadeth me'. Within days George was driving his blue Ford car eastwards laden with luggage. He was descending from the mountain top to the East End valley.

Part Two

SERVICE (1958–1966)

CHAPTER 1

Early Days

A mile to the north of the Thames and the docks stood the May-flower Family Centre, like a shabby fortress surrounded by rows of terraced houses which were broken up by open stretches of debris. Much of the war-time rubble remained, for Canning Town was to be redeveloped as a new housing estate.

George had not yet seen the Centre in daylight and now as he drove into the courtyard he took in the buildings grouped round it. Erected mainly during the 'twenties and 'thirties to provide social amenities for the people of Canning Town, the premises were spread over an acre and a half. In the centre of the garden a fountain splashed into a goldfish pond. To the right a solid beam buttressed the cracking wall of the main club room. A Tudor-style hostel whose black timbers stood out from the white-washed walls formed two sides of the quadrangle. Ahead towered the chapel which seated four hundred, its stained glass windows bearing the coats of arms of the Settlement's titled benefactors.

"How attractive!" was the reaction of most visitors, for it resembled a quiet university college, an unexpected oasis in a grimy desert. But to George the architecture was totally foreign to such an area; it stank of middle-class respectability. He looked up and noticed on the chapel roof the weather vane which silhouetted St. George spearing a writhing dragon—an omen of future conflicts.

He was shown to his room and left to unpack. Some faded cotton curtains flapped at the small, ill-fitting windows which overlooked a depressing junk yard. A high wooden bed, upright chair, table, wardrobe and wicker arm-chair completed the furnishings.

The other staff were busy, so he wandered around. The club block comprised some sixteen high-ceilinged rooms each leading off a maze of dark red corridors. There was a boxing gym, theatre, carpentry shop, open-air playground, nursery school, and a full scale swimming-bath, drained and derelict-looking.

From that first inspection George perceived there was plenty of work to be done. He had been appointed youth leader and was no handyman, but he knew he could make others work. Who was responsible for these buildings, his active mind inquired.

In the club George faced an uphill task. By the time he appeared as the official youth leader the seventy curious teenagers who had thronged into the club a few weeks previously for the opening night had dwindled to a mere fifteen. 'No dancing' meant 'no good' to the girls and there was little else to interest either them or the boys. Besides, the annual fair at Beckton Park which had opened that night was a strong counter-attraction. "Let's go and see the kids at the fairground," George urged Jean. Leaving the handful of youngsters in the club room with the other helpers, they drove off to spend the evening strolling round the stalls and sideshows, observing the teenagers and stopping to chat with the few they already recognised.

By the middle of May the swimming-bath had been cleaned and filled. While the younger club members hailed the opening with enthusiasm, the older teenagers were hardly interested. The boys wanted to play billiards or go out to the cricket nets, and the girls refused to ruin their elaborate hair-dos. Finally George persuaded a tubby girl to take the plunge, and she swam a few lengths to the cheers and jeers of the others. Thereafter swimming became a feature of the club and qualified life-savers were required.

This need led the Mayflower staff to accept offers of help from various well-wishers, among whom were secretaries, teachers, an artist, a doctor and a banker. Club life introduced them to a new world, challenging their values and attitudes. Some came for only a few weeks, and then, curiosity satisfied, or unable to stand the pace, wrote a polite letter explaining why they could no longer come.

One evening David Sheppard brought a tall young man across to the club and introduced him to George. "This is Mark Birchall. He's offering to help, if we can use him." Dressed in city suit, silk handkerchief protruding, rolled umbrella in his hand, ex-Eton and Oxford, it would have been hard to suggest a more unlikely helper. Yet George took to him. That evening he had a long talk with Mark, sharing with him something of his own background and faith in Christ. Mark planned to see more of George Burton and his club.

Unlike others who came wanting to teach and to mould, he was aware that he had much to learn. His first lesson was how to guard his property. His pen and cigarette case were filched and then handed back to him as the club closed with the curt injunction, "Look after yer fings, mate!" A week or two later some Artful Dodger acquired for good his red-spotted silk handkerchief. Fortunately Mark took his treatment in good humour and was promoted to collecting subscriptions.

As numbers increased George became dissatisfied with the rooms they were using. "They're too small and poky," he said. "We must move into the Club House." This largest club room of all had been used as a furniture store since 'Dockland' closed down, but he soon got the young people and helpers shifting tables and chairs and then scrubbing walls and floors. By mid-June the Teenage Club was meeting in this large room, where a quick glance could determine what each member was doing, whereas the rest of the premises required more supervision.

George's influence was creating a new spirit, and in order to foster it he held a barbecue one Saturday night. The garden, where staff and residents kept their cars, and the hostel premises were strictly out of bounds to club members. "The cars can be moved," George insisted. He ordered hot dogs and tea, and had coloured lights hung from tree to tree and a huge bonfire built. Music blared across the courtyard to greet the teenagers as they arrived in high spirits. When darkness fell, George signalled a helper to let off his *pièce de résistance*, a firework display. The club members went home realising that their new leader enjoyed a bit of fun as much as they did.

"Can we have a cricket match?" one of the boys asked him one evening. George found a team to play them the following Saturday. Braces and hob-nailed boots were the uniform, morale was high, and even George enjoyed the game. Violent swipes left wickets undefended and they tumbled rapidly. Honour was maintained by forcing a draw and the team went away well pleased with themselves.

Apart from the club work George's other tasks were not clearly defined. During the day-time he liked driving out to tour the area, taking someone with him, for he never wanted to be alone. Spotting a group of children at play, he would draw his car into the kerb. "Oy—come 'ere!" he would order, "I wanna talk to yer," and in a moment he knew their names, where they lived, and if they ever came to the clubs. If not, he invited them. He made sure they knew his name before they parted, and many a child came to one of the clubs " 'Cos Mr. Burton told me". In this way he found recruits for the younger clubs although his own sphere of work was with the teenagers.

One area which magnetised him was a block of red-brick flats, known as 'The Buildings'. Two or three small shops served this community, for no bus service came within nearly a mile. An expanse of treeless park-land adjoined the estate, but children seldom played out there. They chose to play in the stairways or on the bare asphalt courtyards surrounding the flats. This was the area which reminded George most of Glasgow, and his heart went out to those families, especially the children. He began to pray for an entry into their homes.

One night a pale, thin, serious-faced boy of sixteen came into the club, alone. This was remarkable, for everyone went around in groups of two or three or more. "I'm the leader, Mr. Burton," George informed him. "What's your name?" "Bill Turner."

"That boy is unusual," George told Jean at the end of the club, "I'd like to visit his home." The next time Bill appeared George was intrigued to hear that he came from 'The Buildings'. The following Sunday George went and explained who he was, but Mrs. Turner did not invite him in. "Bill is out," she frowned, shutting the door. A week later George was back again and pushed his way into the home. He gathered that Mrs. Turner had been left by her husband with six children to support and that Bill, the eldest, had barely left school. George's interest was kindled and he started to share the life of this family which reminded him so much of his own childhood. He became a frequent and favourite visitor to the home and began patiently to pray for Bill, whose reserve somehow deterred him for over a year from speaking directly to him about Christianity.

Another area that attracted George was the Rathbone Street

market, known locally as 'Rathy', only a stone's throw from the Centre and the hub of Canning Town life. He loved to stand listening to the slick patter of the salesmen. Many of his club members worked there, and he would go and chat to them, finding out prices and learning their 'fiddles'.

One Saturday he knew distinctly that God was telling him to go to Rathy. As he reached the market he saw a crowd gathered round a policeman. Stopping for a momentary prayer he walked over to them and was told that a small girl had wandered away from her mother and was lost. George learnt her name and joined the search, picking his way through the mud and puddles of waste ground. Then he caught sight of the girl playing happily in a pool of water. He called her by name and stopped to play with her for a few minutes before carrying her back. "Thank God," cried the grateful mother as she hugged her child. "Do you really mean that?" George asked her. And then, addressing the crowd that had gathered round him, George introduced himself to them. He pointed to the Mayflower chapel and said, "Why don't you come to the service tomorrow evening so that we can all thank God together?" No one came, and George soon realised that it would take long personal friendships before people with no church background would attend services.

George had come to Canning Town not merely to run a youth club or make friendly contacts, but to win people to a faith in Jesus Christ. It was his constant prayer that God would give him 'souls'. Within a few months, however, his continual conflicts with many others at the Centre impelled him to resign. He packed his case, jumped into his car and drove off.

As he passed the Lowings' house, he looked up and there was Charlie beckoning him from his window. He had often stopped to have a friendly word with this disabled man and had spoken to him about Christ. He drew up and went indoors. "I want to ask you something," Charlie was saying. "Yes, you want to ask me how you can come to know the Lord," George guessed. And within minutes he had won his first soul. George turned his car back to the Mayflower and hurried to find David Sheppard and tell him the news.

CHAPTER 2

The Staff Team

David Sheppard had committed himself to stay as Warden of the Mayflower for at least ten years and he hoped that the rest of his staff would stay for a long time too. Of the original team, half had left by 1961, but a nucleus of five remained together for eight years. As he considered the failure of the church in so many districts like Canning Town, Sheppard became convinced that a major factor was the sheer loneliness of the single-handed minister which either drove him out or, if he stuck to his post, dulled his thinking or blunted his sense of purpose. But in the strength of a staff team minds could be kept sharp, fresh ideas ventilated, and problems shared.

At first George dreaded the weekly staff meetings held in the Sheppards' flat. He often suspected that the others were sneering at him in some way, and so was usually strained and easily provoked into an explosive outburst. Staff duties tended to overlap and this led the Warden, now known as 'Skipper', to clear the air. "I'd like us each to say what we reckon to be the area of our responsibility." Each member of the circle spoke until they came to George who had declined to speak earlier. "I've been listening to you lot," he rounded on them, "and not one of you has said what you ought to have come here for. I have *not* come here to run youth work. I have come to win souls for the Lord Jesus Christ. I have a great gift for soul-winning and," glaring round the room, "I don't intend to get lost knocking nails into bits of wood." He was referring to the incident when other staff members had joined the housekeeper repairing torn curtains and broken seats in the swimming bath cubicles, and had been irritated by his dogged refusal to help. "I haven't come here for *that*!" he had fumed, as he stalked off to pour out his complaints to the secretary.

The Council members were also watching his behaviour with

some misgivings. At their meeting six weeks after his arrival Skipper gave his report. "He seems to have the confidence of the teenagers, but it has not all been plain sailing in his relations within the family, as he is a person who does not settle easily into a community. It might be best to wait a further month before making a decision about keeping him on the staff."

Despite his own hesitations, Skipper felt increasingly certain that George's gifts could be used in his team and with the Council's approval he wrote to George on July 3rd, 1958, appointing him as a permanent member of the staff. He waited in vain for the note he asked for agreeing to the terms; for George had no intention of tying himself down. He wanted to be free to walk out, and this often happened. The blue car would disappear through the iron gates and head for the West End, though it always returned in the early hours with a calmer, more sober George Burton. Nevertheless he took the precaution of fixing a roof-rack in case he should decide to disappear for good.

The staff members were given a day off every week and left the premises for a complete break. George had few friends to whom he could go, but he continued to see Helena again at her home in Kensington where she carried out her couture. He enjoyed the tasty Hungarian dishes which she cooked for him. Her sister Mariska was often there too, for her husband Peter was now settled in London as a patissier.

Soon after George's arrival the staff began to prepare for a camp in August. They heard of a site on the Sussex coast and George offered to view it with Helena and Margaret Fish, the church worker. A single glance told George that the large field was suitable. It had a water supply and was situated only a few minutes from the sea.

At the next staff meeting George was asked to report, but he gathered that Margaret had already spoken to Skipper about it, so he merely replied, "It's suitable; ask Margaret." Margaret realised that he was annoyed and added nothing. But other staff members were not satisfied and with Skipper's consent visited the site for themselves. George fumed inwardly.

The camp was not a happy one for George. He offended the cook by wandering into the kitchen tent at all hours and demanding pots of tea. "He should be like everyone else and have his meals and drinks with the rest," she protested. The other staff had definite spheres of work and he felt spare. So he lay in his tent and prayed for opportunities to talk to individuals about Jesus Christ.

The first was Ginny, an American student spending the summer at the Centre. She detested his loud, assertive manner, but his talks with her led her to ask him how she could become a real Christian. Within a few years Ginny was serving God in the Far East. Then there was 'Professor' Eddie, an intelligent twelve year old who was full of problems like evolution and the authority of the Bible. George induced Eddie to polish his shoes for him while he dealt with his questions. Jimmy, the youngest camper, had recently lost his father. George went out of his way to befriend the boy and even allowed him to sit at the wheel of his car and drive it round the field.

Yet George's relationships with the other leaders were so strained that David Sheppard himself was now doubtful whether George with his prickly personality would ever settle into the team. At length he concluded that George would have to go; whereupon he spent the most unhappy night of his life. The next day he discussed the matter with Jean who was convinced that George was the right man because his priorities were clear. Perhaps he would manage better if he lived out in digs. Skipper was reassured and wrote to George suggesting this.

George read and re-read the letter. Was this a polite way of giving him the sack? Why had Skipper and Jean been discussing him? He thought he could trust Jean, but evidently not. He would have to cut her, as she and the other staff members had cut him when they had not invited him to a Saturday night social for the younger boys and girls. He was still nursing a grievance over the camp site incident. And now Skipper had gone for three weeks' holiday leaving no address. Angrily he demanded it from Hilary and wrote a letter full of complaints.

Skipper's prompt reply dealt with the list of charges and ended by showing his affection and pastoral care for the 'misfit' on his staff.

"The thing that makes me anxious is that you have been turning grievances over in your mind for so long. In fact once you see things from someone else's point of view you get quite a different picture. I feel that you are tempted to believe evil things of another Christian far too easily. Do read I Corinthians thirteen again—because it's so important for our lives together—'Love thinketh no evil'. J. B. Phillips translates, 'Love does not compile statistics of evil'. 'Seeketh not her own'—not her own importance or good name or rights. If you are puzzled or worried about anything please come straightaway to me and ask me. But not so many 'angry's' as in your letter!

"Others have got to learn to see your point of view and your needs, but you have got to see their problems and ways of living too. All of us have got to learn this lesson."

George apparently took the rebuke to heart, though he always shrank from I Corinthians, chapter thirteen. "It rips me to pieces," was his excuse.

It was several years before David Sheppard could size up his curious associate. George Burton was simultaneously his biggest asset and his greatest liability. He was notably successful in the teenage club and in gaining the friendship of people in the neighbourhood; and he possessed shrewd administrative ability. When the Bursar left, George offered to take over responsibility for maintenanance "as a hobby", and adroitly saved money by obtaining the most reasonable estimates.

On the other hand relationships in the staff team were stormy and all Skipper's diplomatic skill was needed to calm the recurring rows. He had to listen to George's complaints and then bolster his confidence by reassuring him that he valued him as a colleague. Unless he sacrificed precious time for this, which at first he resented, George's work was unhinged.

Two books helped David Sheppard. The first was Leslie Lyall's biography of John Sung, a Chinese Christian. Sung was a man of brilliant intellect and outstanding evangelistic passion and gifts whom God signally used. Yet his marriage was a failure, he spent many years in mental hospitals, and his eccentric, even violent behaviour upset other Christians.

Then in March 1960, *The Daily Telegraph* published extracts from *The Life and Times of Ernest Bevin* by Allan Bullock. The resemblances between Bevin and George Burton were remarkable.

"He had difficulty in writing and read little. He picked up ideas far more from conversation than from reading, using the people he met as other men used books. Most of all he drew upon his own experience. Not only had he great powers of observation and a retentive memory: he continually reflected on what he saw and heard.

"Bevin was often at his best when he spoke on the spur of the moment. He knew instinctively what was in the minds of a working-class audience and the arguments that would tell.

"Conscious of his abilities, he made no effort to conceal his scorn for those who disagreed with him and cared little whom he offended by plain speaking. His prejudices were strong and hard to overcome, and he was inclined to look on anyone from another class as an enemy.

"He was highly sensitive to criticism, quick to resent opposition and to take it as a personal attack. Once he suspected that someone was trying to 'get at him' or down him, he could be brutal in the vehemence with which he hit back."

Skipper asked himself, "If Bevin had been available as a Christian worker would I have found room for him in my team?" Certainly he would have been a painful influence, yet he would have moved mountains. Skipper was finally persuaded that it was right to keep George, and on George's terms, even though the demands on his own time and privacy were sometimes unbearable. A close partnership was formed between them, inexplicable to anyone who saw only their contrasting backgrounds.

Whenever Skipper wanted to embark on a new stage of the work he would discuss it first with George, for he came to realise that without his co-operation the scheme would never be implemented. Besides, he valued George's keen judgment based on his wide experience. George himself was often the one who originated an idea and he would mull it over at length with Jean before presenting it to Skipper. Then the three of them would retire for a day in the country to confer.

Grace Sheppard was excluded from these sessions because

George never felt completely free in her company. Their first encounter was unfortunate. They were walking round the club rooms when George suddenly stepped into one of them and said, "Let's have a prayer." This odd behaviour startled Grace who was recovering from a nervous illness and she could not help showing her fear.

Grace had deliberately set herself not to interfere in the work but was sometimes entangled in situations. Another early incident raised a barrier between them. She once answered the door to a club member and dealt with his inquiry herself without calling George. When she told him about it he stormed at her viciously in front of a crowd of people, "You're just an interfering parson's wife."

When George detained Skipper in his bedroom until the early hours, tracing and retracing his personal fears and anxieties, Grace somehow managed to restrain her curiosity about what had passed between them. The Sheppards accepted George's terror of being talked about and seldom discussed him. At one staff meeting George blatantly started analysing Grace in front of the others. His mis-interpretation of her behaviour made her bristle. "I can't stand people who set themselves up as amateur psychiatrists," she fumed. George retired in high dudgeon, and it was some weeks before com-munications were restored.

And yet there was also a bond of understanding between George and Grace. When Grace gave birth to Jenny in March 1962, no one outside her family was more overjoyed than George, for he had prayed time and again, "Lord, give Grace a baby." He warmly approved of the way she was bringing up the child, even admitting that he could not have done better himself. He loved to sit talking with Jenny, and she became devoted to 'Uncle George'. Once she invited him to a tea-party with her dolls. Setting aside the pressures of his work he gave himself to the child, and for an hour lay sprawled on the floor entering wholeheartedly into Jenny's world.

Of the other staff members George turned most to Jean. He roused her sympathy by sharing with her his secret fears, but then was quick to accuse her of betraying them to others. The shock of dis-covering that she had once tried to explain his suspicious nature to someone so disillusioned him that it took him months to recover. Another cause of friction was a correspondence course on youth work which she was taking, since her essays underlined his own lack of formal education. Yet he needed a woman to talk to, and Jean was a ready listener. He came to rely on her support and encouragement while he dealt with correspondence, phone calls and countless interviews. In the company of others he squashed her contributions, for they might have disclosed his own imagined incompetence; but when they were alone she could tell him things which he could not take from anyone else.

Hilary Harman was the model secretary who remained outwardly unruffled by George's many interruptions of her work.

After a succession of housekeepers the first with whom George was able to strike up a real understanding was Dilys Gething. She won his heart in two ways. At eighteen stone she made him feel positively slim, and she passed with flying colours the interview which he gave her. He conducted it in his flat to test her reaction to the familiar scene of shabby furniture and the dirty crockery left by the young people. She did not blanch. "You can forget all you have learnt about housekeeping," George told her. "We don't want you to run this hostel as an efficient institution, but as a home."

Joan de Torre's appointment as head teacher of the Nursery School gave George the freedom to have a say in the running of the school. The children loved having him play with them and Joan never questioned his visits. From her he was tickled to discover that his theories of education agreed with those of the great pioneer Fröebel.

When David Gardner left Skipper took over all the chapel and mid-week services. But after a year or two the growth of the congregation made the need for a chaplain more pressing. Skipper began interviewing men whose main qualification had to be the ability to 'fit in' with George Burton, and who had to be further limited by having nothing to do with the young people's work. Eventually Hilary thought of a modest ordinand who had stayed at the Mayflower. George excitedly drove up to Manchester to see the Rev. Brian Seaman and meet his wife Marian, and within a few months they joined the staff on George's terms.

Several times a year the staff used the house of some friend in the country for a quiet day. Away from the business of the Centre they enjoyed an unhurried time of Bible reading and prayer. Once George was set to study Philippians, chapter four with Grace Sheppard. They read, "Whatsoever things are true, whatsoever things are honest, whatsoever things are pure, whatsoever things are lovely, whatsoever things are of good report; if there be any virtue and if there by any praise, think on these things." George was ever bewailing the ease with which he fell prey to filthy thoughts. "I'm the worst sinner out of the lot of you," he confessed. The apostle's words suggested positively how he could overcome his temptations. "I think it means," explained Grace, "that the answer to bad thoughts is to put good ones in their place."

George often recalled that explanation. Yet as he looked at his colleagues he believed that, for all their apparent goodness, they too were sinners at heart and that their behaviour was based more on a middle-class upbringing than on their Christian beliefs. The local people noticed that they did not swear, smoke or lose their tempers in public and felt they themselves could never reach such standards. By contrast, George's faults were obvious to all, yet he maintained that he knew Christ and His forgiveness. He kindled in the people of Canning Town an interest in the God Whose acceptance of men and women did not depend on their conforming to a code of behaviour.

To drive home this point George relentlessly exposed his colleagues' faults. "Jealousy, gossip and pride are just as much sin as swearing, gambling and sex outside marriage," he maintained. Once while he was reasoning with a local man, Dick, he sent for Skipper. "Is it right that you and Mrs. Sheppard sometimes have a row with each other?" he asked. "Yes, I'm afraid we do," admitted Skipper. Dick was still incredulous, so George asked Grace to come and corroborate the astonishing fact. "Phew!" exclaimed Dick. "I would never have believed it."

CHAPTER 3

The Residents

In addition to the staff the Centre's hostel housed some twenty residents, thus enabling students, ordinands and others from a different background to gain an insight into the needs and opportunities of such an area. Most worked locally, giving voluntary help in the clubs and in maintenance work. There was, however, the danger that they might occupy key positions for too long and prevent local people from taking responsibility.

From the start George identified himself with the people of Canning Town and saw the residents through their eyes. They represented a Christianity invariably linked with a public or grammar school education, which seemed unattainable to the working man. This was the type who had won quick promotion ahead of him in the Palestine Police simply by having attended the right schools. They were potential enemies, not only to him personally, but to the whole vision he shared with Skipper and increasingly with the staff. The Church in Canning Town had to be founded on local Christians who would work out the implications of their faith in their own way and not be forced to copy the behaviour patterns of these 'supercilious college types', as he termed them.

When a housekeeper bought some practical new tableware, George considered the appearance of the dining-room tables would further discourage local people from having meals in the hostel. Heatedly he dictated a letter to Skipper.

"Where are we spiritually?

"Is the vision that you had at first beginning to materialise?

"Are we really making contact with the local people, getting them into our church, clubs and homes?

"Has the gulf been narrowed between the artisan class and the posh class?

"Did you visualise after three years polished tables and floors, silver-looking vegetable dishes, electric hot-plate, ridiculous fuss on split-second timing at the tables, and air of the aristocracy, our tables set out much different to the way of the local people? Don't you think they are frightened to sit down looking at two knives, wondering which one to use and then wondering what the dessert spoon and fork is doing in front?"

George did not regard the hostel as a retreat where Christians could band together in a sanctimonious clique and have the leisure to discuss 'predestination and election' and like matters. It was, rather, a mission base from which they should launch out to the people of the area.

At first George was regular in his attendance at household prayers, though he could seldom be persuaded to lead them. He disliked the restrictive custom of noting subjects for prayer in a book. One morning the resident who was to lead the prayers arrived late without the notebook. "Oh, I'll have to go and get it," she said. George erupted, "We don't need the book to tell us what to pray for. It's time you learnt to trust the Holy Spirit!"

He hesitated to invite local Christians in to pray with the residents, for he was afraid they would be put off. Once he took the risk, but an earnest resident uttered three long-winded prayers. George's fiery rebuke to the culprit was an unforgettable lesson to be sensitive to the feelings of younger Christians.

When he assumed responsibility for maintenance George needed help for countless tasks. One resident was assigned to renew light bulbs, another to pump and mend footballs; one was told to produce a plan of the entire electrical system, while several others checked scores of locks and keys. In time, with the residents' help, he drew up memoranda on security arrangements, transport regulations, and the positioning and maintaining of First Aid kits and fire extinguishers. He covered the smallest detail because he did his planning on the site and not from his arm chair.

George never forgot the hostility of some original residents towards him. His violent temper and moodiness seemed a bad witness and even posed the question whether he was a Christian at all.

Thinking that they were meeting 'to pray him out', George's sense of persecution prevailed for some years.

As the first ones left, Skipper asked George to share in interviewing would-be residents. He examined their motives for coming, and asked them if they really wanted to have a part in building the local church. "How wonderful it would be," he told them, "if by the end of your time here, you could have brought just one family to the church by visiting their home. Better still, if you could have led one soul to the Lord."

He warned them of the mundane toil ahead of them. "Do you want to serve the Lord? Well, you'll serve Him twenty-four hours a day. So you've got a car? He'll want that too." His chief demand was 'loyalty' even if they did not agree with what was going on. "I may ask you to buy me a loaf of bread," he instanced, "and I will expect you to go and buy it without asking questions. But if I ask you to buy it on a Sunday and that is against your conscience, you must tell me and I will respect your conscience." Theoretically he believed that residents had the right to hold differing opinions, but in practice he interpreted any deviation from his judgement as 'disloyalty'.

As the church congregation grew, more residents were needed on Sundays to mind the smaller children and to clear up the club rooms after the Bible classes. An urgent secretarial job once drove George to commandeer every available resident to work throughout the weekend. A new resident was so upset by this violation of the Sunday rest that he went to see Skipper, and for three hours into the night Skipper talked with him about Sunday observance. When George heard that others too were complaining about the imposed task, he angrily summoned a residents' meeting. "Some of you I stomach. I try to love you but I don't like you. Some of you get up my wick. You are only passing through this place. The staff are staying. While you're here, pick up the good things and drop the bad things. But don't allow Satan to use your tongues. You can do a lot of damage. Satan's at work at the moment, with some of you people nattering. I know every one of your movements in this place. I know the three or four that is not as forward as the others. I know the three or four that is willing to be flogged to death."

George classed the residents as either against him or for him. The former he avoided, for he feared that his animosity might provoke him to violence though a verbal barrage was enough to scare some who roused his anger. But many recognised George as a man whom God was using. They admired his love for people, and his zeal in soul-winning. They were prepared to be ticked off for being 'backward in coming forward' or 'laxadative' [*sic*] and still carry out his orders, often without receiving a word of praise, but knowing that he would not miss a detail. He repaid them by making them realise they were playing a vital part in the growth of the local church, and several treasured personal letters he wrote to thank them for their work.

By his rough but kindly treatment George helped many to overcome shyness. At a resident's twenty-first birthday party he came to the rescue of several non-dancers by teaching them the palaisglide. To him there was nothing questionable about a few dances on such an occasion. He showed a deep understanding of people's inhibitions and problems and loved to know that they were confiding in him, particularly about their romances. He was uncannily observant about friendships. At a meal with sixty people present his evening was spoilt by noticing that a certain couple whose courtship he had encouraged were not sitting together. More than once he booked tickets at the Albert Hall to give a couple a night out, and generously lent them his car.

But he could also be ruthlessly cruel in condemning a friendship, and one who failed to invite him to her small wedding reception received a venomous attack that could have ruined her day.

George liked to feel that he was developing the residents' characters, and several parents were impressed by his swift assessment of their sons' weaknesses and glad of his offer to train them. He profoundly influenced numerous men preparing for the Church's ministry by helping them to give priority to people. Once a resident rushed to his flat in the early hours of the morning to tell him that a pipe had burst in the swimming bath and the situation looked serious. "Try and deal with it yourself," George told him; "I have something more important at the moment." He was deep in conversation with a boy he had been concerned about for months, and shortly afterwards he helped him to faith in Christ.

One new resident was always at the centre of an amused audience enjoying his witticisms. George watched him for some time and then broke in. "Why do you have to play the fool all the time?" he asked him. Then he delivered a lecture on the psychology of clownishness and warned the young man not to go through life branded as a clown. Another winced at his command, "Look me straight in the eye, son. Don't shuffle about from one foot to the other. Hold your head up and be a man!" These experiences were abrasive but salutary.

Of many who passed through the hostel a small handful became George's aides and were brought into his confidence. He needed someone with him all the time making notes to help cope with the sheer volume of administration. If these men failed to carry around sheets of paper clipped to a board and have a pencil handy they would be scolded in public. Frequently he would summon them to 'tour the premises', inspecting the fabric in detail and planning how to use different people to decorate or repair corridors, rooms, furniture and equipment.

Bob Shepton was the first of a succession of 'right hand men', and it surprised others that George could tolerate such public school types. Bob's easy-going friendship meant much to him in the early days. Later when George had to go for a few months' break it was to Bob that he turned for his stand-in.

David Hewitt stayed the longest. Fresh from reading classics at Oxford he came for a year's experience before theological studies. His artlessness irritated George so much that he decided to ask Skipper to tell him to leave. His only hesitation was that he had heard David pray for conversions, and so he himself spent the best part of a night praying for him. David too was troubled, for he knew he had offended George and sought reconciliation. So early in the morning he went to George and found him praying. "Come and join me," George said, and the two men knelt together. As a result David became George's companion and assisted him unquestioningly, by fixing up tape-recorders and ciné equipment or writing lists of points and notes for talks. So useful was he that George induced him to stay for three years.

Others followed and each was given the tiny room near George's

The Rev. Prebendary C. C. Kerr

Portrait of George by
Reg Fleming, 1953

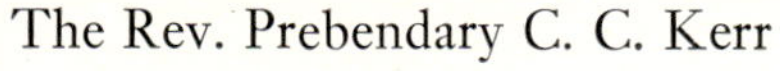

The Regent Restaurant, Blandford Street, W.1

Mannequin Parade at the Garden Party, 1961
Jim Gosling assisting, far right

George Burton with David Sheppard, 1965

flat so that he was readily available to accompany him into his bedroom which he still dreaded entering alone. He also needed someone there while he got into bed, and the aide was usually the unsuspecting chaperon.

George seldom slept well, for his active mind schemed through the night, and his aides became accustomed to being woken up at any time to pray with him and listen to his plans. One was tiptoeing up the creaking stairs at one a.m. when George called him to his room. The table, desk and chest were piled with papers. "I need your help," George appealed. "I want you to take some notes for me." And the next three hours were spent in hectic note-taking until the mountain of paper had been reduced to an orderly list of telephone calls to be made and points for action. Then they adjourned to the kitchen for a huge bowl of cornflakes.

The experience of working with George taught these men resilience and flexibility, loyalty and ready obedience to authority, and indelibly marked their future lives.

CHAPTER 4

The Youth Club

The mixed youth club soon became known in the East End for its lively spirit. George was at his happiest during club hours and his presence was everywhere. He refused to tie himself down to collecting subscriptions or issuing equipment, for he had to be free to talk to individuals, commenting on the girls' new clothes and hairstyles, the boys' jobs and court cases. He usually held his conversations in the corridors with others milling around, though sometimes he would just sit in a chair in the main room and wait for different ones to come and chat to him. If he sometimes muddled their names he knew nevertheless who they were, and their mates. He liked to speak to whole groups together, making sure to acknowledge the leader.

George did not enter teams for sports competitions for several reasons. He knew it took time to run a team efficiently and would not trust another helper to do it. Then he feared that sports might dominate the club and the team members become an exclusive clique. Once he did let a group of friends form a football team for a season but ensured that their loyalty to it did not whittle away their interest in the club as a whole. The club had some of the best boxers and footballers in the district, and the facilities for training them, so George was under great pressure to alter his policy; but he wished to help the boy who would not fit into neighbouring organised clubs. His chief reason was that too keen a competitive spirit might detract from the club's spiritual aim. He once told his club helpers, "The more I look at things, the more I realise how true the Bible is when it says that Satan is the prince of this world. He will use all sorts of wiles to deviate you from your work. He will make you preoccupied with the wonderful football team you are running, or the fact that your team came near to winning the table tennis championship. He will make you want to be sure that the next year they come out top, actually winning the cup!"

Despite his distaste for competitions George encouraged the boys to play football in the open air playground and the two halls. Dozens of panes and a good many frames were smashed until wire guards were erected. Later he set aside a 'beating-up room' filled with punchbags, mattresses and cushions. Skipper wisely left the youth work in George's hands though he did once ask him to accept the offer of a basketball coach. George reluctantly agreed though he considered the game similar to netball and therefore 'cissy'. He never encouraged the boys to play and after a few weeks the coach lost heart and stopped coming.

George adhered to the opinion that cricket was not a game for the working-class man. He saw its value as one of several activities within the club, and the occasional friendly match provided an outing. Skipper backed his policy and, despite his international reputation, was prepared for his skill to be almost neglected. Twice, however, he led a week's cricket tour in Sussex with a group which George was developing.

The cricket match against Slinfold, David Sheppard's home village became an annual event. One year they were stuck for drivers, so while the team gathered George rallied a few friends to pray. As they finished praying four young men arrived to visit the Mayflower—all drivers and all free for the day. George filled his car with girls and the white flannel trousers. The match was already in progress as he sauntered up to the pavilion, ostentatiously licking an ice-cream. The village supporters were watching their local hero silently, almost reverently, and they clapped politely as Skipper hit a boundary. "This lot need livening up," muttered George, and brazenly bellowed out, "How many goals have you scored, Skipper? Come on, Canning Town!" Disregarding the shocked stares, he urged the girls to don the white flannels. "It's too late for the boys to wear them," he said, "and there's nothing else for you to do. You'll get as bored as me watching this stupid game."

In the club he incited the boys and girls to chase each other up and down the corridors. Once the girls' screams were shriller than usual, so he went to investigate. It appeared that a boy had thrown a billiard ball across the club room, narrowly missing a girl's head. George stooped to pick up the ball, and saw staring up at him a slimy cow's eye. It had been thrown by a butcher's assistant.

Another time a gang of boys managed to tie a girl to a ladder and carried her out screaming into the street. Not surprisingly George received a typed letter from a visitor to the effect that she would not be returning again. "I was under the impression that I was coming to a decently run youth club, but I discovered that it was a den of maniacs."

George wanted the members to decorate their own club room. So he detailed two helpers to balance on upended wooden bedsteads and scrape the ceilings. Activities carried on around them but their efforts stirred an interest. "Who'll give a hand?" George asked at last and there was a chorus of, "I'll help, Mr. Burton." A dazzling white ceiling and walls transformed the room and the canteen counter blazed bright red barred with black stripes. One boy offered to mend the wooden panelling behind the canteen, and as he surveyed his finished handiwork he noticed an obstinate nail sticking out. " 'Ere, go in!" he ordered, hammering it flush. A jet of water shot into his startled face, for the nail had pierced the water pipe.

Two years later a smouldering fire charred the whole clubroom. Far from being disappointed at the dereliction, George saw the chance of fashioning an even better room from the wreckage. Assembling the dismayed members he challenged them to set about re-decorating it themselves. He investigated canteen equipment, steel shutters, false ceilings and concealed strip lighting. He re-designed the room, organising the removal of a wall here and the erection of another there. More important than the improved décor was the raising of morale through the success of their efforts.

Early on George recognised the value of transport in extending the Centre's work. He brought the coach regularly to the club door to take the members out for an hour's drive. He obtained free tickets for shows, and the annual outing to Bertram Mills' circus was a feature of the club. The members were more interested in Olympia's side-shows than in the performing animals, but when the blonde trapeze artiste appeared they rallied back to support her with their catcalls. For the final bare-back horse-ride for members of the audience Sid was over the rails like a shot. A crane swung him aloft and gave him contact for a brief second before he slithered off to the delirious cheers of his Canning Town fans.

After one such outing, as the coach returned through Parliament

Square, Pete leant out of the window yelling so heartily that his false tooth shot out into the gutter. They circled Parliament Square once more, but their hoots attracted the attention of a policeman. "Do you realise," he started pompously, "that you are in the 'eart of the metropolis?" Then flourishing his notebook he proceeded to list the points in which the coach was defective. Thereafter George was careful to check its lighting, number-plates and general maintenance.

George was not concerned merely to run a successful club. He constantly kept in sight his aim of winning boys and girls to a faith in Christ; so that for him the key activity was the weekly service. It took considerable skill to ferret the members from every corner of the rambling premises and make them sit down half-way through the club evening to listen to a talk. Before coming to the Mayflower George had had little experience of speaking publicly about his faith. At first he relied on others, but several failures by visiting speakers, moved him to speak himself. He realised too that the youngsters had to hear the gospel from people they already knew like the chaplain, Jean, one of his aides or other residents.

Even Skipper who came in to speak every few weeks could not at first hit the right wavelength. Once he was telling the story of Margaret, a fifteen year old Christian who died of cancer. He spoke movingly, describing the way in which the lump in her side grew larger and more menacing. But it was clear that he was no longer holding his audience. They were giggling at a girl called Margaret whose tell-tale bulge declared her state of pregnancy.

The reason for the happy club spirit lay largely in George's relationship with his members. Many confided secrets to him that they would never have shared with their parents. He liked to be asked to help those who were in trouble with the police and he became known in the local courts for his statements on their behalf. He deliberately set one group of potential young criminals the task of decorating three club rooms, so that he could mention this fact in their favour when, as inevitably happened, they were picked up on a theft charge.

Of the boys whose records indicated that they were heading for a life of crime George kept in touch with as many as twenty over a period of five or six years. He believed that they could be changed only by the power of Jesus Christ. Yet he was prepared to be patient.

Kevin was the eldest of three brothers who had all had convictions. Notwithstanding George's report Kevin was sent away to an approved school and George used to write to him. Just before his release he obtained permission for the boy to join a holiday in Belgium. He believed that Kevin would respond to this special treatment and keep his contact with the club on returning home; but his faith was disappointed. Another boy, Ron, was leader of a tough gang. When he claimed at a camp that he was a Christian, George encouraged him on but also advised him to stay with his mates with a view to winning them too.

One night a crowd of excited teenagers bunched round the club door watching a car swerving across the road. It lurched to a halt and two figures ran from it. George cleared the teenagers into the club and sent for the police. As he walked towards the abandoned car he noticed someone dive into it and dash out again as the police car approached. The boy tripped and the policeman grabbed him. It was Archie, whose record George well knew. In a flash George identified himself with Archie and sprang to his aid. "I saw two other boys getting out of the car," he offered eagerly. "It wasn't this one who stole it. I know him and I'm prepared to go to court for him." But the young constables were unimpressed; they had captured a boy they had seen at the wheel of a stolen car, and they hustled him off. George was furious, and when one of the helpers told him that she could testify to Archie being the reckless driver, he shouted, "I don't *want* to know what you've seen." Nevertheless, having received this damning evidence, he could only write a letter to the court instead of appearing in person.

George never hesitated to call the police if there was any trouble which looked dangerous. "They must learn to respect the Law," he insisted. Almost invariably he dealt with the matter himself before they arrived, and only pressed a charge as a last resort.

He believed in making the young people's acquaintance outside the club walls and often stopped in the streets to talk to them. Once as he stood on a pavement chatting to two club girls he noticed some shop assistants giggling at him. He stormed up and reprimanded them, "You think I'm just a dirty old man, but I'm a youth leader and they are my members!" In one club member's home the mother was ill and a mound of clothes was waiting to be ironed. George loaded them into his car and set half a dozen Mayflower people to iron them.

At the Turkish baths on his day off he mixed with bookies and dockers, poultry merchants and traders, and as he listened to their uninhibited conversations he learnt much about East End life. At a local billiards hall he met several 'self-employed' young men whose names were well known to the police.

As a rule George discouraged visitors to the club because he did not want the members to feel under observation. An exception was the local youth officer who had won his respect by her diplomatic interest in his approach. When Sir John Hunt came one boy greeted him unceremoniously, "Oh yeah, you're the geyser wot climbed Everest, ain't yer? Well, I could 'ave dun it meself if I'd 'ad the roit boots on!"

As the club developed George built up a strong team of helpers most of whom came for an evening a week. A number reached a faith in Christ through their association with the club. Interviewing a would-be helper, George asked, "Are you a Christian?" "That's for you to find out," replied the young man. "I've already found out by your reply," George rejoined. "Anyone who knows Christ isn't ashamed to say so."

He won the affection of many attractive lady helpers to whom he was charming, deeply understanding and completely open in discussing intimate details of their love affairs. City bowlers and college scarves were anathema to him and he was cautious of helpers with too much personality who might tug the members away from himself. He had a nose for lesbians and homosexuals, making sure that none returned after their first night.

A new helper was critical of the apparent lack of discipline and suggested that the members should be organised into teams with captains, as he had experienced in the house system at school. George listened attentively. "Look here," he broke in at last. "*I'm* the leader here and I shall run the club the way *I* want. I don't need your ideas or anyone else's. If you don't like the way I'm running things, get out."

Once a year he organised a meal for his helpers at a 'Chicken Inn', after which he would deliver a carefully prepared speech.

"When reporters write about the work here, it is Skipper that is mentioned, and I have sometimes been jealous of it. But you know that the one really in charge of the youth work is myself, and God has used me, and we are seeing many battles won: but where would I have been without you helpers? It doesn't come easily to me to say thanks, but I want to assure you that I do appreciate what the majority of you have given; and that has been loyalty."

However much George depended initially on his outside helpers, his aim was to train the young people of Canning Town to run their own clubs. Meanwhile he looked out for local adults who would serve at the canteen or help with other activities. Jim Waller first came to the Centre through an invitation to a home meeting. He had a church background but it took George to win him to a personal allegiance to Christ. His wife Ethel was so shy that she seldom left their flat. George took up the challenge and to Jim's surprise she agreed to try helping at the club. George escorted her to the canteen, artfully removed her coat and left her. If she had been able to find her coat she would have walked out within a few minutes, but after surviving her first night she stayed for years.

Another local helper was Grace Spencer whom George first noticed at a church service. He started to visit her home and inveigled her husband Tom to supervise the boys in mending broken furniture. As an experienced joiner Tom shuddered to see them hacking at plywood with choppers and was indignant at the deliberate damage to the furniture. But George showed him that the boys were more valuable than the chairs and he too became a regular helper.

Jean was running the junior girls' work, and as girls' leader shared leadership in the Teenage club. At first George seemed to need her opinions and discussed all plans with her usually late into the night after the club had closed; but later he resented any suggestions and she was slow to accept her changing role.

Once a visiting party made the mistake of referring to Jean rather than George, and this triggered off a wave of suspicions about his colleague. He dealt with her in the only way he knew: he cut her dead. As certain business needed to be discussed, she made various approaches to settle the misunderstanding but was bluntly rebuffed. They both spent a painful few weeks before communications were resumed.

But George believed that others too were against him and that Skipper wanted to be rid of him. He took the initiative by telling the staff he would be leaving. Skipper heard the news while he was away for a few days and wrote immediately.

December 17th, 1959.

"My Dear George,

"Hilary has mentioned that you told the staff you would not be with us in the middle of January. This has upset us both not a little. Whenever you and I have talked about it, you have agreed: 1. That God called you to the Mayflower and, 2. That He has not called you anywhere else. There can be no greater sin than deliberately doing something which takes you out of God's will. Armies rightly regard the greatest crime for a soldier to be desertion in battle: yet this is what you are telling your fellow-soldiers that you propose to do.

"I cannot possibly encourage you to consider leaving us. I would have as much right to encourage you to go and commit adultery. You have got to put the temptation resolutely from you; to make up your mind that you will not leave; that you will not say that you are going to leave to others, until and unless God calls you very plainly to another work.

"You know how much we both value your fellowship in the work. Do put this aside as what I am convinced it is—a temptation from the devil—and let us get on into the battle God has called us to.

"Our love to you,
Yours as ever,
David and Grace."

George treasured this proof that he was indeed wanted and valued in the Mayflower army. He tucked the letter carefully into his back pocket.

In December 1961 the junior boys' club leader retired and was replaced by Michael Miller who came from the National Training College for Youth Leaders at Leicester. His qualifications made George uneasy, but Michael's steady competence was a big asset and George soon handed over leadership of the Teenage club to him, while keeping his own overall authority. By the time Michael left two years later George was involved with other groups, and so he ran the clubs through a succession of deputies. But it was never the same without his presence and interest.

In terms of numbers of conversions the club was not a striking success; but it was a valuable means of becoming acquainted with young people of the area and then communicating with them. And in fact many who passed through the club did later become Christians.

The Sunday Group

Other Christian youth leaders pointed out that their two main problems were how to obtain and keep club helpers, and how to present the gospel intelligibly to teenagers. George resolved to train his own leaders from club members. As for evangelism, he realised that on the whole the club members were not responding, and so came to reckon that intensive work with a small number was the most effective way. He was given a two-roomed flat on the top floor of the hostel and began to pray that God would show him which ones were to be approached and trained.

In the summer of 1959 he collected about a dozen boys and girls and invited them to meet with him on Sundays. None were chosen for gifts of leadership or other obvious reasons, but, he claimed, at the prompting of the Holy Spirit. They came at two p.m. and piled into his car and a borrowed Dormobile for a drive to Epping Forest, Blackheath or the West End. Once a chauffeur-driven car trailed them, unable to pass on the congested road. The youngsters waved cheerily at the passenger, a dignified bishop. His grim face illustrated their own impression of the Church and goaded them to grimace instead. "If only he knew the value of a smile," George reflected.

Back at his flat George provided tea and sandwiches before the evening service, attendance at which he made the one condition of joining the Group. "They'll only come to the service as a group," he calculated, "and when other young people see them they will want to come too." At the time the congregation, apart from residents, numbered only some twenty adults, mainly elderly. Anticipating the young people's uneasiness he insisted that the adults sat near the front while he reserved the back rows for the young people. There they were more free to whisper or pass round sweets. They were nevertheless heard by all, and Mrs. Olley, for one, was roused to turn round and 'shush' them.

As soon as the service was over they charged back upstairs to the flat. After another cup of tea, some thumping on the piano, much laughter and fighting their leader settled himself in his green leather armchair and demanded silence. As they sat around on the window-sill, piano and an assortment of half-broken chairs, George would toss out some provocative remark to start a discussion on sex, race, attitudes to parents or Christianity. Particularly skilful in drawing out shy ones he controlled every moment with masterly ease and informality. In one such discussion they agreed to adopt the name 'The Sunday Group'.

In August George and Jean took six of them to Blankenburge on the Belgian coast. The party included three boys he was especially cultivating, Jim Gosling and Len Howell, and Bill Turner, the boy from 'The Buildings'. Much of the holiday was spent in the bed-room, where he lay in bed for hours recounting his experiences and eventually steering the conversation to Christianity. He consented also to display his wizardry with a pack of cards.

At other times they strolled along Blankenburge's gay promenade and into its back street shops; they climbed the bell tower at Bruges and sniffed disdainfully at its fifteenth-century houses; they made a trip to Dunkirk. But George was not stimulated until he noticed a signpost to Meli Amusement Park. There he forgot every-thing else as he licked ice-creams, played with chimpanzees and filmed flamingoes. His ciné camera appeared everywhere. "You'll enjoy looking at yourselves in a few years' time," he prophesied.

Back at the Mayflower he held a social evening so that parents and relations could see the holiday film. He had already visited all their homes, for he was determined to influence not only the young people but their families too.

In the autumn of 1959 George opened his flat to the Sunday Group on several week nights as well, for he wanted them to regard it as their home. Though they continued to attend the teenage club, they could sit talking more freely up in his flat. One evening Len stooped to turn up the jet of the gas fire when someone touched his ear with a lighted cigarette. He leapt up with a yell, deliberately kicking the fire in anger. The door opened and Mr. Burton walked in and, taking everything in at a glance, slipped out again without a word. It was some weeks before the subject was even mentioned.

George was prepared to tolerate other inconveniences. Having recently given up smoking he loathed a smoky atmosphere; yet there was no protest when they sat on his bed stubbing out their cigarettes on the headboard. Then he discovered lice in his hair, caught from one of the boys who sprawled on his bed, and had to resort to the local clinic.

Although as few as two boys and one girl were committed Christians they all enjoyed singing hymns. Just play the piano," George told Jean. "Don't say you can't." One evening as they sang their favourite, 'Jesus Christ is risen today', Len was studying the words and knew he did not believe them. He guessed that most of the others did not either. "Yer just a bunch o' 'ypocrites, the lot o' yer," he shouted abruptly, and stamped out of the flat. Walking home he began to regret his action. "I can't go back there now," he thought. "Mr. Burton won't want me after that."

Hardly had he reached home when Mr. Burton appeared on the doorstep, scarf twisted round his neck and hands stuck in the pockets of his old overcoat. "Whatcha, mate," he grinned; "want a polo?" Pushing his way in, he went on, "You were good in there tonight, Len. You had them all shocked," and he laughed at the recollection of the outburst. Len chuckled too. "Come on back," urged the leader. "I don't care about what you said. You're probably right anyway." And Len, subdued but knowing that he was accepted, returned.

George never forgot his main aim of leading these young people to commitment to Christ. Weekends away were opportunities for the Group to think more seriously about His claims. But George's unorthodox approach scotched co-operation with other youth leaders.

In October he took some of the Group on a joint weekend and, in the presence of qualified youth leaders, was edgy and critical from the start. Bill, Len and Jim were sharing a dormitory with some others. "Where are your pyjamas?" one of them asked Bill, who had never worn a pair in his life. "What do you want pyjamas for?" George chipped in. "We don't wear them, do we?" He knew his boys felt out of place and when Len refused to go in to one of the sessions George approved. Lights were meant to go out at ten thirty p.m. "Lights out in ten minutes," announced an officious voice. "They will *not* go off in ten minutes," broke in George Burton, who suddenly appeared, and added, "they will stay on till four in the morning if they want." Emboldened by such disaffection the Canning Town boys prolonged their laughing and joking, and prevented the others from sleeping. Trying to apply some restrained psychology one of them wearily inquired, "I say, old chaps, what do you think you are trying to prove?" Jim's retort was triumphant: "Well, it's keeping you awake, isn't it?"

George knew that he had to run his own weekends. But where could he have complete freedom? He heard of Ashburnham, a mansion in Sussex, and without prior reconnaissance arranged to go there. But the first weekend brought difficulties, as he poured out in a letter to Skipper.

"I feel that I must get some things off my chest. Ashburnham is a wonderful place but it is only suited for the good boy. John Bickersteth could not have been more co-operative and I know that I am looking for the impossible from other Christians when I take the East End teenagers out camping. I find that I am up against a code of behaviour that is expected from the grammar school and above type. If I spent my time watching that the tent pegs did not get broken and the boys cleaned behind their ears and cleaned their teeth, did not eat sweets before their main dish, and concentrated on teaching them to respect other people's property and was continually apologising for their noisy behaviour and the unseemly mannerisms and teaching them to say 'thank you' and 'very sorry' and getting them to fit into a pattern that middle class Christians have laid down, then I would not be doing the job that Christ has called me to, and that is seeking for the opportunities to speak about Christ, and also to train young Christian leaders.

"I realise more and more that I have to be tolerant and accept the fact that the majority of Christians only care for the good type of boy and girl. I thank God that He has called me and some others to care for those that some could call the unlovely.

"Was the Lord's Name spoken of?—yes. I had a long talk with Pat Deadman and others and I thank God for a wonderful time round the fire on the second night talking about Christian things. I honestly believe that the Lord was at work and that we shall see the seed of that camp growing."

In the coming months the seed did grow and bear fruit. The patient prayerful approach resulted in some of them turning from apathy or doubt to faith in Christ. George took every opportunity to single them out with a view to counselling them. He even took one or two with him to his West End osteopath. He had suffered discomfort ever since a bottle hurled by one of the club members had caught him on the neck. As the specialist's manipulation reached a climax George's companions would cheer him on, "Come on, Guvnor, knock 'is bleedin' 'ead off!"

Bill's rare remarks at their discussions indicated that he was thinking deeply. George found it inexplicably difficult to talk to him about Christ but he prayed for him and in time Bill quietly committed himself to the Lord. Len was another. George had noticed a change in his attitude, and one weekend his challenge, "I believe you are a Christian, Len," drew the confession that he had been one for some months. By the summer of 1960 Jim Gosling, too, declared that he was a Christian. George enlarged the Group with several younger brothers and sisters and other friends.

Jim was thick-set, assertive, determined and eager to learn. George had always seen him as the future leader of the Group and spent many night hours with him. "I believe you are going to be a preacher, Jim," he prepared him. "Now, let's see if you can talk for four minutes about this pencil." Much to his own surprise Jim was able to discourse on the manufacture and function of pencils. George longed that the boy should be freed from the terror of speaking with which he himself was still haunted, and he gained a vicarious pleasure from watching Jim's development. Jim had to be not just a good speaker, but another Billy Graham.

George was ambitious that Jim should take out the Group in the Mayflower's old coach and so he detailed people to conduct him driving until he passed his test. Other potential young leaders followed and George lent his car for driving lessons unstintingly. When he realised that neither Jim nor Len could swim he made out that he himself was a novice. Jumping in first, he instructed them until they could swim easily. Both boys continued to practise judo, the activity which had originally attracted them to the youth club, but George ruled that they were not to achieve high grades merely for their own satisfaction, but in order to pass on their skill to others.

These young Christians needed to grow in their faith, so George started a weekly Bible study for them. Instead of letting the brightest ones forge ahead and leave the others discouraged, he planned that they should develop as a group. He considered that they would learn more from studying the Bible together than individually, so he did not stress the absolute need for daily private Bible reading. However he gave a copy of the New English Bible to every Group member, inscribing in each book their name, his own signature and a text.

Despite his rule of church attendance George did not fully support the principle of corporate worship, and this weakness showed in the development of some of them. "Two or three meeting together in Jesus' name are a 'church' just as much as hundreds going into a special building," he contended. He seldom sat down for even five minutes of the evening service, for he undertook to welcome newcomers, to engage in conversation with passers-by, now and again enticing some to join the service, and to control the growing number of noisy teenagers who attended. He would even prowl in and out during the first half of the Communion service to see if any late-comers were hesitating to come in and needed to be escorted to a back seat. He still had qualms about accepting the cup of wine, but did not discuss his views with the young people for fear of confusing them with his doubts.

He was anxious to see his converts become full members of the local church, so he waived his uncertainty about the Church of England and encouraged them to be confirmed. To fill in their lack of Christian background Skipper drew up a thirty-week syllabus. "They'll never stick it out that long," George objected. "Besides, they're getting teaching from me in the Bible studies in my flat." After the first year Skipper agreed to cut the course down to a mere six lessons. George's mixed feelings towards confirmation itself were reflected in his attitude towards the classes. One year he pressed some twenty teenagers to attend, chasing them up if they missed a

Field-Marshal Montgomery visits the Over 18s Club, 1959

George with David Hewitt in Jerusalem, 1965

The first four couples of the Sunday Group: Jim and Janet, Alan and Rita, Bill and Doreen, Len and Pat

George with David and Grace Sheppard

The Mayflower Staff Team: *Back row* (*from left*): George Burton, Margaret Fish, Dilys Gething, Joan de Torre. *Front row:* Jean Lodge Patch, Hilary Harman, Grace Sheppard, David Sheppard

week. The next year he reacted, "To heck with it. Let Skipper go after them himself if he thinks confirmation is so important." He mentioned it to no one and only a handful of teenagers went forward.

By early 1961 there was a sufficient number of Christians in the Group for George to give Jim the responsibility for which he had been pining. He put him in charge of a team of seven to run a club for boys of eleven to thirteen. George intentionally dropped his young leaders in at the deep end, but he was always standing by in case they floundered. Sometimes one of Jim's helpers had a romance, or a row, and failed to turn up, and it was to meet such contingencies that George insisted on a team of helpers. A team was also needed when the boys ran wild along the corridors. Once Jim was showered from above through a hole in the glass-panelled floor. "That's someone piddling on me!" he guessed, rightly, and bounded up-stairs to clear the club. The retiring boys hurled bricks and other missiles at the steel-lined doors. After a year's experience Jim was ready for promotion as leader of a larger team of Sunday Group helpers to run a new 'Young Teens Club'. Scorning a whistle with which to call silence, he raised his voice and yelled for order, just like George Burton. "We run this club to tell you lot about Jesus Christ," he proclaimed. "If you don't keep quiet while we talk to you, well, we just pack you up—chuck you out. It's as simple as that. Now, listen . . ." and for a few minutes he would speak to them about some aspect of faith in Christ, still fresh to him, which he was keen for them to share.

Jim's progress as a club leader made George glow, but he realised that club work was not the best way to train most of his young people. He could give responsibility to a greater number of the Sunday Group by breaking the youth work down into small groups, each to be run by two or three leaders. But this task would have to wait until he had taken a well-earned break.

CHAPTER 6

Interlude

The Mayflower Council realised with David Sheppard that it would take many years to establish a truly local church in Canning Town. To keep staff members fresh for the long-term work, they arranged to grant each one a paid long leave every few years. By the summer of 1961 it was George's turn and he planned to visit his brother Bob who had emigrated to Canada when George was a boy. He could muster little enthusiasm for the trip until David Hewitt offered to go with him. This put the holiday in a new light; for a 'chaperon' might ease him away from the lure of women and gambling, to which he feared that by himself he would have fallen prey. George also formed some positive resolutions: they would read the Bible and pray together daily; they would seize every opportunity to speak to others about Christ; and through their experiences he would attend to broadening David's education.

On the plane to Montreal he lost no time in opening a conversation with an attractive Greek student; and, prodding David to switch on their portable tape recorder, he expounded to her the necessity of being 'born again'. The frugal hospitality of their first hosts stunned George. With every item of food rationed there was never enough to satisfy their appetites. They were expected to share a double bed, which George let David use while he slept on the floor. During the hot night he rolled off the blanket to find himself stuck to the polished wood. Yet he was able to regard the hardship as a test of faith and, instead of complaining, laugh.

George had bound Jean and others to write regularly, and he thirsted for every drop of news. In reply he sent tapes emphasising sensationally that God was giving him the best of everything. "It's wonderful, out of this world, you couldn't describe it," he enthused.

If the provision was God's, the determination was certainly his own. When he heard that Roy Rogers, the Christian cowboy film star, was speaking at a rally, George was bent on going. Arriving late at the stadium, they gathered that 12,000 had already been turned away. "But I'm a youth leader, I've come from London," he remonstrated brandishing Mayflower leaflets. "I don't care if you're the Mayor of Los Angeles," came the reply; "you're not getting in." George sat down mopping his brow. "God hasn't brought us here for nothing," he claimed, "and I believe He will get us inside."

They pleaded, chatted, prayed and waited, while an hour and a half passed. By the time George prevailed upon the Chief of Police to admit them, the rally was nearly over. They stood in a corridor behind the main platform and as the celebrities stepped off George pressed one after another to speak on tape and be photographed. Finally he caught sight of Roy Rogers with his wife Dale slipping away behind a curtain. George was not beaten. Tearing through the curtain and pursuing them along a passage he pleaded breathlessly, "Please will you send a message to my teenagers in London." George posed for a photograph with Roy and Dale who told how they had come to be fired with a love for children. Next morning George recognised Jayne Mansfield at the airport and secured another interview and the inevitable photograph.

His brother Bob, was unmistakably a Burton. Stout, homely, blunt and coarse, he could both draw tears of laughter and scare the victim of his hot temper. His boasting could evoke ridicule, yet his tenderness could win the affection of the shyest child. To the citizens of Creston, British Columbia, he was known as 'Pop'. "What you don't see, don't ask for," he growled, as a generous mixed grill was planted before the weary travellers. The two brothers were bound to quarrel, for each was striving to impress the other. But the eruptions quickly subsided. Over religion they found more points of agreement than disagreement, and the whole family united to sing hymns and choruses. Before one meal George's grace lasted so long that 'Pop' had to rescue the burning pancakes.

From Creston George and David were aiming for Vancouver. But the news of teenage riots at Spokane across the American border aroused their curiosity. The riots were quickly suppressed, but Spokane's 'skidrow' provided some pathetic spectacles. Drunken wrecks staggered up to beg from the prosperous strangers. They passed a sign, 'Alcoholics Anonymous—Fellowship Group', and went in. There was a bar at which soft drinks and coffee were being bought, and the walls were labelled with proverbs. A few men sat around in silence. As George began to ask questions the barriers fell and several told him how they had managed to stop drinking with help from the 'Higher Power'. When George was called upon to speak about his work in London, he made it clear that anyone could know the Higher Power personally, as he did, by believing in Jesus Christ. One of the men, Wilbur, questioned George afterwards and recounted his own story of struggle and failure, in and out of prison. "I didn't want to come here tonight; I intended to go out on the bottle. An alcoholic is lonesome and full of fear. What would an alcoholic do in church? There would be no one to talk to, he would be out of place."

George made up his mind to sacrifice Vancouver for Wilbur's sake. Meanwhile he was annoyed to discover that David had run out of tapes. David also showed his annoyance. The heat, the travelling and the strain of each other's company bred irritation. Somehow they bridled their tempers and avoided separating. Throughout the day and into the night George continued to reason with Wilbur until at one a.m., as he prayed, Wilbur at last encountered Christ.

Some months later Wilbur wrote to thank George. "You gave me a few hard hours. You broke this old fraud of an ex-convict and alcoholic into small pieces. Thank God you don't give up easy." By his persistence George had far exceeded the limits of courtesy; but someone had been needed to push Wilbur into committal.

George knew there was truth in Wilbur's objection that an alcoholic would not be accepted in church. He knew also that they were not the only unacceptable ones. He had heard about Toronto's interdenominational People's Church, described by some Christians as 'eccentric'. Yet he attended a service there with eight hundred working people and at its close several walked forward in braces and shirtsleeves to record their allegiance to Christ. George's vision of a working-class church was renewed. He set his heart on preaching as effectively as the minister, Oswald J. Smith.

George had always assumed that preaching was limited to men of education. But why should not the rule be broken? At four a.m. one morning he read a tract and then woke up David to announce that he wanted to record a sermon on tape. Bleary-eyed, David prayed that the batteries would not be flat. The result was certainly animated, though lacking clarity and coherence. For George it was a triumph: he had produced evidence that he was a preacher. He dispatched the tape for the private hearing of Skipper and Jean.

George had not been away long before he felt homesick. From the Mayflower he heard something which money could not buy, that he was being missed. "For all the comfort and wealth out here I would rather have Canning Town any day," he declared. Besides, he was anxious to see to his car which had developed another rattle. He was infuriated to learn that this car which had been used so much for the Lord was valued at only ten pounds.

In his restlessness he covered in under two weeks San Francisco, Los Angeles, Dallas, Chicago and Washington. The various sights could not hold him for long. From one place he reported to the Sunday Group in a bored voice, "We have done what one is supposed to do here." It was people who appealed to him. There were the children in a park with whom he pranced about in a wild game, gathering them round for a story, to which they listened with open eyes and open mouths. There were the boys whom he teasingly refused to pay for cleaning his shoes. That set off a playful scrap from which George emerged with a sore neck and empty pockets. There were the two ladies, elderly and staid, whom he insisted on calling 'young ladies' and whom he 'interviewed' as if they were racing drivers. "Now of course there is only one Effie . . ." he began. They adored it.

George used the tape recorder as a tool of friendship, for he was expert at eliciting people's views. He was interested in coloured people and had no qualms about conversing with an educational psychologist. "We have something in common," he confided. "You see, I'm interested in psychology too."

Visiting the home of an economical missionary he asked himself to tea. Before her startled eyes he deliberately consumed a whole pot of home-made strawberry jam. His compliments, however, disarmed her utterly and made her feel it had been her privilege to entertain George Burton. A variety of people found it easy to confess to George their secret problems. He was a good listener and they in turn could listen for hours while he uncovered some of his own weaknesses and then dug down to the root of the trouble. Married couples were amazed to find that after a slight acquaintance he had spotted the causes of friction between them.

On arrival in New York they received messages from the Sunday Group. "What-o, you pair. Well, you monkeys. We've painted the coach. I painted the engine-top and the dashboard. I'm still making a nuisance of myself. We are praying for you as I know you are praying for us. I am a good girl, I went to church this Sunday." Jim was learning leadership the hard way. Only seven others had come to help him re-decorate the flat; and when he rebuked the rest some had refused to listen. But on the following evening everyone co-operated and Jim could report, "It just shows what prayer can do."

In New York it was 'freedom at last'. Being a guest in strange homes had been a strain for George. So they lived in cheap apartments and observed the city's life; young people drifting, flirting, gambling on street corners; stout, swarthy housewives from Spain and Italy; the police, casual, gum-chewing, lacking authority. They visited a Harlem youth club run by Jim Vaus, a converted gangster, and George approved of his method of concentrating on just a small group of gang leaders.

Street corner speakers abounded. George listened to a controversy between an open-minded Jew and an aggressive Christian addressing each other simultaneously. The Christian broke off to distribute tracts, then darted back to quote verses from Isaiah and to brand his opponents as 'brainless dopes'. The battle thickened as the champions hurled at each other quotations from Pliny, Josephus and Philo. George stood between them restraining hecklers and trying to see fair play. He corrected a Hebrew word and silenced a drunken Irishman. A teenage gang threatened to break up the gathering until George first called on the ringleader to make a speech, then used him to dismiss the others. Finally he gained a hearing for himself and declared how much Christ meant to him.

He told the Sunday Group that he was 'not too excited' with New York. The skyscrapers awed him, though the height of the Empire State Building discovered his cowardice. He was not fit; his neck called for constant massaging, and he developed a boil on the stomach. As he rested he would ask David to read out long passages of the Bible, which he punctuated with questions. Then they enjoyed a home-made meal at which they did not need to submit to any conventions.

A sea journey to Tangier gave George further rest. He took advantage of the large crew, demanding that meals, cups of tea, pills and other requirements be delivered to his cabin at all times. There was always something he wanted which was not on the menu, always a niggling complaint. "God owns the world," he argued as he sampled every comfort, "so I'm sure He wants Christians to enjoy themselves sometimes." He obtained an interview with the captain and was photographed steering the ship. A fellow-passenger gave him a guarantee ticket for a trip to the moon.

His moodiness expressed inner conflict. He ached to write down his life story. It could interest and help others; but, more than that, he sought to view his life objectively, to understand his own character, motives and actions. But he could not write unaided. Was he ready to entrust David with the secrets of his murky past? He was alarmed that his own consequent fear of betrayal might sour their friendship.

He planned to initiate David by degrees. Arming him with biros and papers, he pledged him not to ask questions, comment or divulge a word. After David with due solemnity had assented, George lay down and dictated the story of his early life. A start had been made.

At Tangier George remembered his fluency in Arabic and caused the citizens to stare in wonder, then grin with delight. He demonstrated how to bring a vendor down to a third of his price. George was enthralled by the sunset flight to Madrid. And there was Helena running to meet him. He had asked her to join him for a brief part of their holiday and the three of them went on to Palma where they rented a modern flat overlooking the gay harbour. While Helena was busy preparing delicious meals, David assisted and shopped, and George rested. He reasoned that if Helena were like himself, truly 'born again', then a happier relationship would necessarily follow.

George boasted that he could run his Mayflower work from Palma. He flooded Jean with directions and requests. He even began to be grateful for her letters and conscientious tackling of responsibilities and admitted that it was only his own jealousy which stopped him entrusting her with fuller authority. He was suspicious about Bob Shepton reading the Bible with his own protégés Jim and Len, although Bob assured him that it was not 'college stuff'. He was also annoyed that Jim had formed a committee out of his helpers in the Young Teens Club. For the coming Annual Meeting George specified which local people were to be invited and who was to travel in the dormobile. He also pondered about the future now that some of the Sunday Group were looking forward to marriage. How could they be inspired to make their homes in Canning Town?

He believed however that God had given him leisure in Palma for another special purpose. He had to complete what he had started in mid-Atlantic. David had arranged and rewritten the notes, but the mood for writing had not yet descended upon George, and time was running out.

Money was running out too, for expected reinforcements did not come. They were reduced to angling invitations from acquaintances and opening tins of sardines. On the day before the flight they had only nine pounds between them for their journey home. George spent an hour haggling over the price of air tickets and managed to save ten shillings. Later, when they went to say farewell to an evangelical minister whom they had met, George felt constrained to give him some three pounds of their precious money.

Next morning on their way to the airport they called to see if there was any mail. George opened a letter from David Sheppard advising him to stay in Palma a little longer until he was fully fit. Then there was a cable for David from his bank advising him where he could collect fifty pounds. "What a wonderful God," George acknowledged, and cancelled the air flight. They installed themselves in the luxurious Bahia Palace Hotel.

George knew then that he had to write. With David's notes and constant company he scribbled furiously for two days, finishing with a burst from two to five a.m. The hundred foolscap pages represented one of his biggest achievements. Having conquered that summit he was ready for whatever trials lay ahead at the Mayflower.

CHAPTER 7

The Group Idea

Back at the Centre George rededicated himself to training the Sunday Group for Christian leadership. His definition of a leader confused some, for he meant simply a committed Christian who was prepared to accept responsibility for running certain activities for young people and share their faith with them. Small groups of teenagers were to be the channel for this service and evangelism.

But first he had to handle an influx into the Sunday Group of some thirty boys and girls. They were taken from a close-knit group of girls and a similar group of boys, both of which were now to be disbanded. In January 1962 George called them together and invited them to become members of 'The New Group' which was to meet in his flat. He outlined his vision of their future merger with the Sunday Group and of how eventually they were to become leaders of other groups too.

His invitation was not greeted with enthusiasm, for they resented the closure of their clubs and he did not know them sufficiently to have won their affection. George was hurt by their disgruntlement and hit back. "It's easy to cut yourself away from those you don't like and make a little clique. You've got to learn to mix with everyone, in the Teenage club and in my flat."

Initial jealousies between the two groups were largely overcome during the summer holiday when he took the combined group of some sixty to Blankenburge. Anticipating difficulty with a few girls who had not accepted his leadership he refused to take them. His ruthlessness was a shattering experience for them and they were lost to the Mayflower for good.

Throughout 1962 the idea of other younger groups was never far from his mind and he pored for hours over lists of boys and girls, their ages and addresses. His pretext for asking someone to accompany him to his room was, "Come and run through the lists with me." Gradually a scheme crystallized. Six new groups of thirteen and fourteen year olds would be created, three for boys and three for girls, and from them would be drawn the future recruits for the Sunday Group and later the future leaders. Each group would be run by a team of two or three Sunday or New Group members, with Jim Gosling taking overall supervision alongside Jean and himself.

George unfolded his plans to some twenty Group members individually to awaken their interest. Then in November he called a meeting in his flat. "The New Group doesn't exist any more," he announced. "You're all the Sunday Group now. I've given you all a lot of time, love and understanding. Now I want to see you giving the same to others. Some of you are already running clubs. Others are going to start taking responsibility in these new groups. Still others I regard as potential leaders."

For the next hour he outlined his vision, sharing with them the gist of his four year 'Schedule for the Birth of the Fifty Leaders'. But it also expressed his awareness that human planning was subject to God's will. "Who knows what the Lord has in store for us? How wonderful if we should have a pouring out of the Holy Spirit and in fact see 500 leaders by the end of 1965, and how much more wonderful if our Lord Himself should come."

The six new groups containing some seventy young teenagers opened with a flourish. One group began by decorating the club room in which they were to meet. Others used the redesigned staff flats equipped with gas stoves for cups of tea. The youngsters played records and table games, and had discussions. They would also go off for other activities such as swimming, and the boys were allowed under strict supervision to sample the new rifle range. On the first joint outing for all the groups one of George's dreams was fulfilled as he watched Jim drive them away in the old coach. He arranged also a New Year's party, an outing to the West End, a day's trip to Oundle School and a weekend camp for all the group members.

He initiated meetings for the young leaders to report their experiences and problems and to pray together. For this purpose he transformed a room of his flat into an impressive 'Operational Room' like the one at the Police Headquarters in Jerusalem. One wall was covered by a huge calendar showing all the activities, films, camps and outings worked out for the various groups. Another outsize chart listed the group leaders with the names of every boy and girl in their charge. A set of coloured filing trays was made to hold his circulars to the leaders. The room was also intended to be a show-piece for visitors who could view at a glance the whole sweep of the Mayflower's work. A circular chart four feet high depicted the programme from the Nursery School to the Grandfathers' Club. At the hub of the circle stood out the text, 'Ye must be born again'. "Unless we see conversions all the rest is useless," George postulated. A club helper, Vic Mead, was enlisted to draw a map of Canning Town and paste it over the entire ceiling. "This is our target," George announced: "to win Canning Town for Christ."

The stimulus of the regular meetings and George's inspired oversight bolstered the morale of the young leaders. "You will have achieved something if you have only four left in your group by the end of the year," he encouraged them as he listened to their reports. He urged them to know their members individually. "How wonderful if you could win them for Christ," he enthused, and was eager to hear of any conversations about Christ and the Bible.

George was always ready to expound the group idea. "Few people can handle a crowd," he explained, "but anyone can run a group. All they need is a home and a vision." He visited a local school and the next day some of the boys arrived at the Mayflower to form a new group. George started a pillow fight in the garden and they decided to come again. Within a year several of them had become Christians.

Then there was the Camp Group.

> "It is mainly to follow through the seventeen who professed Christ at camp. They come from six till seven, have a swim, muck about for a bit and for ten minutes someone will speak on the Christian life or on something about the Bible."

The camp he mentioned was held in Billericay at Whitsun 1963. It was the first full-scale Mayflower camp for which George had been responsible, and the keynote was freedom. He reluctantly inspected the tents daily by way of encouraging a group of troublesome older boys to whom he gave the highest marks. Discovering that they had taken some camp beds from the stores tent, he did not rebuke them but sent for two more for those who had failed to acquire one. Then he settled in their tent for a talk about Christ.

Rosemary Finch was a resident who later joined the staff as a youth leader. She was a keen supporter of the group idea and was willing for George to advise her about her Guide company. "We've been here five years, Rosemary," he challenged. "We should have produced our own captain and lieutenant by now. Where are they?" Any potential leader had left the Company long before she was old enough to accept responsibility. "I don't think you will keep the Guides unless you offer them something extra," came his advice. "I'd like you to run a group for them after their meeting. Let them change out of their uniforms and enjoy themselves in your flat."

George was unable to be with them on their opening night, so he taped his talk to them. "Why shouldn't you grow up wanting to help other young girls in the Guides?" he exhorted them. Three months later he was visiting them at their weekend camp. "Isn't it thrilling?" he dictated. "Most of them are now coming to church and they didn't come before. Two of them are going to confirmation classes and four others are wanting to know about Christ." Within a few years two of them had warrants as lieutenants and one was training to be captain.

The Sea Scout troop was composed of eight or ten unruly boys. "If we can't produce leaders from this lot we might as well pack them up," George declared in the spring of 1963. "I want to turn them into a maintenance group instead of scouts. They've done so much damage that it's time they did something constructive instead." He ran the group through Ted Lyons, a Sunday Group member and recent convert, but continued his own supervision and set them to work papering the hostel. "Fancy the East Enders decorating the college types' residence!" he chortled. Other jobs followed, but paint and brushes had to be removed immediately afterwards or else the surplus would be used to splash slogans on doors and walls.

George looked for opportunities to talk to them individually about Christ. Charlie knew it was his turn when George singled him out to play a round of clock golf on a day's outing at Southend. There on a park bench he committed himself to Christ. Bobby too became a Christian, and when he heard the astonishing news that his brother Arthur was wanting to follow suit, he exclaimed, "I bet the ole devil will do 'is nut!"

A year later George could write, "My answer to anyone who criticises the closing of the Sea Scout troop is this: except for one they all profess Christ." When they asked to be confirmed by way of confessing their faith George felt his patience with them had been worthwhile; but then their pranks raged worse than ever. Since they came when no clubs were being held, they had the run of the premises and in one evening smashed seventeen panes of glass in the carpentry room. Another night as they leapt from roof to roof, Peter tripped and dangled from the guttering before being rescued. Other leaders wondered how much longer George would tolerate behaviour that would have barred any other boy from the club for months.

Ignoring the havoc George kept appealing to the good he saw in them. "I need some help getting the tents up for our weekend camp," he told them. "We'll go as the advance party," they offered. He let them sleep in the club room before setting off with him at dawn. By the time the others arrived the tents were erected. George seized on this opportunity of congratulating them.

On their promotion to the Sunday Group they left their distinctive marks upon his flat to the disgust of everyone except George. Yet even his patience was exhausted when on a weekend away he recognised their handiwork in wanton damage to the bedsteads. Quivering with rage he confronted them with the incident in the presence of the whole Sunday Group:

"I've got a wonderful club and you're all welcome to that, with all your filth and dirt. I don't believe there is such a word as 'unclubbable'. But you come to my flat by invitation. This is my home and because I've been prepared to give it to you lot, a number of you have come to know Jesus Christ.

"How many rules do I have? Only three: no drink, no familiarity in the flat, and you come to the church service. I'm not so worried about rules getting broken, but I'm concerned with the people that's breaking them. I believe you as people matter a thousand times more than the chairs and windows that get damaged. But I'm telling you now I'm not taking any more of your mucking about.

"There's some of you here taking the blood from me and all you do is spit and swear in my face. From now on you'll either fit in or get out."

For a time they conformed, but to his great disappointment he never saw the fruit which he had in faith claimed from the Maintenance Group.

The Sunday Night Group originated with the teenagers outside the Sunday Group who were flocking to the Sunday evening service. Their wild behaviour led George to appoint a committee of the toughest of them, on the principle of setting a thief to catch a thief. With masterly diplomacy he levered out their sense of responsibility by collecting their suggestions for enforcing discipline in their group. "You need boundaries, Mr. Burton. You don't want people running all over the place. You can't have them mucking about in the T.V. room." "What if they do?" George asked. "We'll give them a right hander!" volunteered Billy. George had succeeded in bringing over the worst offenders to the side of the law.

The Guitar Group met on his day off, but George often paid them a visit to bellow into the microphone, 'I belong to Glasgow'. One Christmas he pushed them forward to play at the Carol Service. The result was an unforgettable rendering of 'Silent Night', played at full blast with two amplifiers reverberating the beat round the low-ceilinged temporary chapel.

George was unable to sell his group theory to everyone. The 'records, muck about, and cup of tea' programme hardly sounded educational enough to the heads of local schools when George suggested late afternoon groups for the senior pupils. Nevertheless an increasing number of people sought his advice. "Don't copy me," he warned, "if the Holy Spirit isn't leading you. One room is enough to run youth work. But there's a cost attached to using your home for Christ. If you aren't willing to give time, love and understanding to young people, and put up with a bit of damage, don't start at all."

His interest was roused in a neighbouring church with only a handful of teenagers. He inspired them with the idea of belonging to a group meeting in a cellar under the vicarage. He freed a Mayflower resident from other duties to establish this group of teenagers who as individuals might have dropped away from the church.

When two girl residents left for Australia he stirred them to believe that they could use their flat in an inner city area to create a group. For two years he corresponded with them about their project. "You should be making contacts with the young people who you are going to invite into your home, and be visiting their parents regularly." Finally he urged, "Don't forget the vision."

CHAPTER 8

The Crutches Go

This flurry of activity over the new groups coincided with a period of extreme personal tension for George. From his past record he might have been expected to leave the Mayflower after a year or two and go abroad; but he battled courageously through the next tempestuous months. While he needed others in countless ways, his two main props were Skipper and Jean Lodge Patch. They understood his weaknesses, so that he could count on them to stand by him when the pressures became unbearable. By 1962 it was Skipper's turn for a long leave and he decided to spend it playing cricket on the M.C.C. tour of Australia for which he had been selected. How was George going to manage with Skipper away for nearly a year? As Skipper's departure in September approached, his anxiety came to a head.

In August he reported to Skipper from the Mayflower camp.

"I personally have led five young fellows to the Lord, and seven other campers were also won. Thrilling! Wonderful!

"Things are going exceptionally well, but the devil has had many attacks and I am sure he is not going to stand back, and before long there will be a big attack."

George was leaning more and more on Jean, insisting that she should remain with him continuously; and she was freed from other commitments to be his aide. Knowing that George could not function without such support she came to accept her passive role. But when her father went blind Jean consulted Skipper about leaving to look after him. She indicated the possibility to George, who delivered his ultimatum. "If you go, I go too." He was frantic and bound her to stay with him all evening. For the first time his behaviour scared her. He locked the door and hysterically threatened suicide.

Before he sailed, Skipper advised Jean to have a break to make up her mind. Jean's letter telling George of her decision to leave dismayed and angered him. He dictated a letter to Jack Wallace the Council's chairman and retired to bed.

October 9, 1962.

"My two crutches have been knocked from underneath me, and I am now resigning—something I have been wanting to do from the day that I came to this place."

For the next few weeks George locked himself in his room and kept dosing himself with pills. David Hewitt remained with him day and night. He bombarded Jean with a succession of typed letters, pleading, cajoling, menacing.

From Australia Skipper kept writing to support George:

October 14, 1962.

"For me one of the great reasons why God has brought me on this tour is because in a settled job like ours I can get to lean on the staff and the regular routine of life there rather than on Him. He will not allow you to be tested above your powers.

"George, I think I know just how great and real your fears must be: I suppose they are of yourself and of other people's judgements. He would never have allowed the two crutches to be taken away from you if He wasn't going to provide all the help and grace that you need. I believe the Slough of Despond is one of Satan's greatest weapons to make us give up."

Jean eventually agreed to compromise and work part time at the Mayflower, on condition that George saw a psychiatrist. Her decision released him to plan ahead once more, and he wrote to Skipper about the seven young people who were the first of the fifty young leaders he was aiming to train.

At the end of November Jean's father died. For George this meant one thing: Jean's immediate and full return. The prospect spurred him to renewed action. He issued a letter to all the club helpers with an invitation to join a course he was organising for them in the New Year and an explanation of the Mayflower's vision of local leadership.

Jean however was not so sure. She had been able to view the

10

Mayflower objectively and was hesitant about resuming the oppressive partnership. She knew that George envied her qualifications and she thought he would get on better with someone he could dominate more easily. Astonished at her delay George asked Skipper to press her to return full-time.

Later he wrote to Skipper about the painful strains of December.

"My eldest brother Tom, from Glasgow died, and with Jean persisting that she would not be coming back, I then planned to move out and officially announced my resignation. The Devil had me right down but somehow I still believe that God had His hand on me and David Hewitt never left me.

"Then came Christmas Eve with over forty of the Sunday Group at a Christmas dinner prepared, cooked and run by them, and three minutes before I was due to sit down at the head of the table, I was told that my brother, Bob, in Canada had died—my two brothers within a couple of weeks of each other. Instead of announcing my resignation I spoke about the Lord Jesus Christ and how he had defeated death.

"I was in a terrible state and I packed my things and got a bed-sitting room near one of my Bridge clubs in Bayswater. I felt that Satan had to be defeated by Jean coming back to work together with me."

Her indecision tantalised him. She *must* come back; this was his sole thought. He needed her help for the book he aimed to write. He had proposed joint authorship, but she knew the ideas would all be his and had declined. She had to be made to feel indispensable, not only to him but also to the developing work. George outlined for her eight grandiose projects for the coming months. They included chartering a boat for a week for 600 church members' families; chartering a plane for the various groups to Palma or Blankenburge; courses for the young leaders and helpers; and sending out teams of witness accompanied by the Guitar Group. The letter ended, "Yes, plenty to do and I know that God has given me the ability. I don't flinch from the work but I won't stay on here without you . . . If only you would come back and allow the work to continue."

In the New Year he wrote again.

"COME BACK, there has been a change in me and I am prepared to alter more. I can go to bed at night without someone being there, tidy my tables and I don't hit back like I used to do. Admittedly I am typing this letter for I have still got the fear of . . ."

Never did he reveal the word 'writing'. He added that he had arranged to see a psychiatrist. At his first interview, however, he resisted any attempt to probe his problems and failed to attend again.

It was mid-January when Jean at last made up her mind to return full-time to the Mayflower. He poured out his relief to Skipper.

"We have a wonderful Saviour and since I have known about Jean coming back, I am fully on the ball again. I am prepared to continue this sixteen hours a day and no days off.

"P.S. Recently I have prepared a lot of points for *My Book* 'Five Years as a Christian Youth Leader' or 'The difference Between a Youth Leader and a Christian Youth Leader' or *perhaps TWO BOOKS*."

For this book George dictated dozens of headings to David Hewitt and then told him to write all he could on each subject. David knew George well enough by then to express his thoughts.

In his absence Skipper's substitute was the Rev. Richard Allen, lately Warden of St. George's Crypt, Leeds. George took to both Richard and his wife Mollie, for they were unaffected by his attempts to shock them. Mollie, a doctor, recognised his anxiety state and took a sympathetic interest in him. "Richard and Mollie couldn't have fitted in better," George reported to Skipper. "He takes a back seat and is willing to push forward the likes of Jim and others." At one staff meeting Richard dared to crack a joke at George's expense. "Mr. Allen was facetious to me and I stood up and told him so, but he apologised three times so I swallowed and sat down."

George was far-sighted in preparing for Skipper's return. He realised that people would compare Skipper's meaty sermons unfavourably with Richard's amusing, though instructive, chats.

"You are only passing through the Mayflower," George told Richard. "Skipper's here to stay, and you're not being fair to him. You should preach longer and duller sermons."

Grace Sheppard had confessed that she was feeling "rather frightened about coming back and wonder how I shall fit in." George understood her alarms and reassured her. He added, "Please, Grace, make sure that Skipper keeps a freeish diary, and that he keeps some time for you and Jenny. We are all looking forward to seeing her. We remembered her first birthday and we pray for the birthday when she is born again." At the same time he urged Skipper, "You have got to be with the local people especially when you get back. I will be glad when you are back."

Despite the nervous strain George enjoyed shouldering the extra responsibilities. He was sure Skipper would be pleased with the progress. "You will notice terrific strides forward. We are now seeing between twenty and thirty more young people in the church. The majority of my leaders will pray aloud now and I am going to try to bring in a time of corporate prayer with the older members of the church. I shall try to get the adults to accept the younger people and vice versa. Unless they mix now I can see difficulties later on."

But George wondered if he was slanting his reports to show off his own ability. He told a different story in another long letter of March 21st, 1963.

"Satan has been having a terriffic go and the people who seem to be upsetting things are the Christians.

"On Thursdays we have the Guides group meeting and Ted Lyons and his Maintenance Group. I have three residents laid on to assist. But practically every Thursday I have had to be here myself because something has gone wrong. Tonight I went across and saw the boys. Ted was late again and the boys were annoyed because there were no jobs laid out for them and the club room wasn't open. They had been waiting half an hour, one of the residents didn't turn up while the other two were having good old 'Christian Fellowship'.

"Ted still helps run the group but is slipping away. Jim has been up and down a few times in the last few weeks.

"A number of the residents have been nattering again.

"A number of the group go out drinking, a couple of the girls especially are going in the pub. The Guitar Group has broken up. Alan Smith, the leader, was given a very big beating by some of the club members who are now after the others in the group so they are keeping away.

"Sheila who is becoming one of the best leaders had trouble with her two deputy leaders. For that matter there has been trouble with the majority of the leaders in one way or another.

"There were three fights in the flat the other night. Two *Christian* girls were pulling each other's hair, lying on the floor screaming—how *wonderful*!

"We are still in the red and there is a possibility of a dozen residents leaving in September.

"There have been three lots of money stolen in one week.

"Bill Turner is thinking about joining the R.A.F. Frances is away from home.

"A lot of these upsets have rubbed themselves on to me and I an telling you straight that sixteen hours a day is getting me down. I know that I am sinning in not taking my Thursday off but I have found that Thursday has been my best day for getting things done."

The gloomy phase passed and the next letter was in parts more cheerful.

"The ceiling of the temporary chapel is nearly finished. The Nursery School children and the Tinies Club are lined up, along with the Mums, to do some painting this week. Thousands of pounds' worth of work has been done. The club premises are more or less being redecorated by the teenagers. Clubs are good. You can hear a pin drop in the Teenage Club service.

"The leaders have just finished running a very successful weekend, but the best news of all is that another soul has been won. Jaqueline, aged seventeen, who has been coming to the Sunday Group since you went away accepted Christ with tears in her eyes, the record player blaring away, a cup of tea in her hand and one in mine as I sat opposite her.

"I am very surprised that you don't comment on my writing a

book on five years as a Christian Youth Leader. Somehow I thought you would be behind it.

"I can't find words to express the fact that J.L.P. is back again. I won't say that I am fully well for I have had a horrible time, yet somehow I keep working.

"As I write this letter I am really down and I feel I must get away from the Mayflower. David and I are going off. As yet we don't know where to but I think I have got to get out of England. I realise this is a crucial time but I also realise I am not well."

Within a few days George and David were in Davos, Switzerland, armed with the 150 pages of notes David had written. Feverishly George rewrote them, adding a few insertions and dispensing with headings or breaks. It was above all this task of writing that had taken George to Davos.

After reconnoitring in Italy for a Sunday Group tour, George wrote down a story in which he tried to express his writing phobia. It was about a couple on a desert island who worshipped an unknown deity they termed 'Penno'. He posted it to Jean who promptly acknowledged the strange essay. Her letter missed him, for he decided to return a day early and phoned at midnight asking to be met at the air terminal. Assuming he had received her letter Jean made no comment at that late hour about his writing. George deduced that she disdained his efforts and this supposed rejection plunged him into agonies of doubt. Jean was unaware of his suspicions but became apprehensive of his dangerous behaviour. Afraid of violence she disappeared.

While she was away, her letter which had missed him in Switzerland reached him at last. So she *had* written after all, and she thought his writing was good. His relief was intense and he hastened to type her a letter of apology. Jean returned, but conscious fear had driven a wedge between them and their relationship could not be the same. Her absence during the year had forced George to turn to others for support; while the removal of his other 'crutch' for ten months had fortified his authority within the staff team.

CHAPTER 9

King Pin

The Sheppards returned in July 1963 to find George Burton's influence stamped on every aspect of the Centre's life. Staff meetings had become a means whereby he could control decisions of all kinds. Having seen the need for total co-ordination he ensured that he was the one who held the reins. "I'm not a dictator," he would explain, as if to forestall critics, "but I *am* a leader, and God has given me a terrific ability to organise." It seemed to some that it was George Burton who ran the Centre rather than David Sheppard. Skipper was prepared to let people think this, so highly did he esteem George's talent. And he knew both that this dynamo worked best when given a free hand and that George did in fact respect him as the Warden and had already proved his loyalty.

George, however, guessed that Skipper would want to assert his authority again and oust him from his new position. So he sought to test Skipper's attitude towards him, and in particular looked for a word of congratulation for the hard work he had put in to improving the buildings. He had for instance organised the repainting of the lofty chapel walls in a single week. He borrowed some scaffolding, gathered twenty teenagers and sat in a pew directing operations while they slapped two coats of paint up to the rafters. And yet the Warden was not even taking the trouble to notice all he had accomplished. Was he jealous? George stored up his rancour and saw slights where there were none. When Jean defended Skipper he even suspected them both of ganging up against him. Fearing that he might 'blow his top' in front of local people he arraigned Skipper privately. "Why haven't you thanked me for all the work I have done? Do you resent my work with the adults? Do you want me out?" David Sheppard's astonishment was unconcealed. Grieved that he had not sensed George's alarm earlier, he offered his apologies so genuinely that George's accusations melted away. They knelt and asked God not to let misunderstandings split their partnership.

To reassure him Skipper granted his request to be known as Deputy Warden. The first time he took the chair at a staff meeting in Skipper's absence, the others arrived late; so George, interpreting this as disrespect to his authority, abruptly cancelled the meeting.

In his eminent position he was more nervous of being made to look ridiculous. He relied on retainers to corroborate his statements. He relied on Jean most of all, but he feared all the time that she might make some deflating remark. Once while he was outlining some grand project, she had chipped in, "Have you only just thought of that?" "How did you guess?" he rounded on her. The incident, trivial in itself, was the source of considerable uneasiness.

There was now nothing that lay outside his range. Catering, cooking, cleaning, all passed under his scrutiny as he devised means of economising. As early as March 1961 he had told Skipper, "I wish you would draw attention to the Council that the round polished table that they sit at when they have their meeting costs the Mayflower about £25 a year to keep clean. Kate spends well over half an hour per day polishing that table. I have actually timed her."

Transport was a constant headache, but George was indefatigable in keeping cars and coaches in good order and in training drivers. When someone offered a yacht to the Centre George unashamedly told him a coach would be more use. Moved by such forthrightness the man handed him a cheque for £500 on the spot.

As Senior Youth Leader George took oversight of every department of the youth work. He disapproved of the uniformed organisations owing allegiance to an outside authority and, having turned the Sea Scouts into a maintenance group, closed down the Cubs. The results of this decision were painful, for it caused friction with the two Cub leaders, who were faithful church members.

He often called on the Brownies and was enrolled in turn as Pixie, Elf, and Fairy. He organised a party for them and asked the maintenance boys to mimic a pop group while he led the Brownies in waves of delighted screaming.

Ever since Joan de Torre arrived as Head teacher in September 1962, George patronised the nursery school. The children accepted him as a friend who was ready to romp with them or sit quietly watching them, and he particularly liked to spend time with a shy child. He inspired Joan and her assistant to use the school as a strategic link with the children's homes. Joan asked George to help her run a parent-teachers' meeting. "I said some general stuff about the Mayflower," he informed Skipper, "and then took them for a flying visit all over the premises and it was wonderful to hear their comments."

During Skipper's absence George thoroughly surveyed the Sunday School work, blatantly disrupting lessons to enable the children to move around. "I'd like to see them enjoying themselves on a Sunday morning," he declared. Once he slipped into the boys' Bible class while Colin their leader was praying. When he stopped George strolled to the front. "How many of you understood or can remember what Colin has just been praying about?" he asked them. No one stirred. The experience was shattering to Colin but made him realise the difficulty of holding the boys' attention for long stretches.

Such fact-finding inquiries made George question the very principle of Sunday School teaching. He shared his misgivings with Skipper who agreed wholeheartedly and, after discussion with the rest of the staff, gave George freedom to initiate changes. Having gained the interest and co-operation of all the teachers, he delivered to them the fruits of his thinking. "We keep saying at the Mayflower that we have got a vision—to build a church in Canning Town. This must be done by local people themselves, not just the blue-eyed boys who wear badges and quote texts correctly, but those who trust in the power of the Holy Spirit more than their education."

Then he spotlighted their motives for undertaking the work. Were they doing it for Christ, he probed. Elaborate visual aids could be designed to promote the artist's self-importance rather than to instruct the children. As for the content of their teaching, "We have got to teach sin, repentance, coming to Jesus." Disliking the restriction of a syllabus he told them to use any current affairs to illustrate divine truths and to rely on the guidance of the Holy Spirit. Leaders and children favoured the new approach, because with more freedom everyone enjoyed the meetings and the children listened better. Later on a weakness was revealed in the lack of direction George gave the leaders about their lessons. He did not appreciate the difficulty of finding fresh material each week and the children missed a broad and solid grounding.

Skipper was convinced that it was necessary to win the men of Canning Town as well as the women. Early on he had opened a men's club, but the members, being unsympathetic to Christianity, refused to accept any conditions imposed by the staff and resented their interference when they tried to mix with them; so after two years Skipper closed the club and waited for a nucleus of Christians. Some years later he held a specifically Christian monthly meeting in his flat, called 'Men of the Mayflower'. George considered his young leaders were receiving sufficient teaching through the Sunday Group Bible Studies and so was half-hearted in urging them to attend.

The Grandfathers' Club had always interested George but it was not until December 1961 that Skipper asked him to assume responsibility for it. He worked through deputies but would often wander in for a game of billiards with the old men. He knew of only one conversion through the club and this endorsed his aim to concentrate on young people. "It's hard to turn to God when you're old and set in your ways," he held.

The older women had an afternoon meeting which George seldom failed to attend for a few minutes to chat with most of them. "It is very important that you squeeze the old dears' hands," he would instruct ordinands. "When you get your dog collars on, they'll be queueing up at your churches just for that." Once he drove them all out to Epping Forest and persuaded them to play a football match while he filmed them.

He always had a word with a bespectacled old lady with curly black hair. "That cough mixture did me a power of good, Daisy," he said. "Thanks for bringing it." And then he announced to them all, "If any of you have a cough like mine"—he demonstrated—"try some of Daisy's mixture."

Margaret Fish, the church worker, ran the younger wives' meeting and George did not at first feel free to join them. But he chose to do so when Margaret was away. The visiting speaker had just embarked on her address when George burst in and took over. "Hello, Mums!"

he greeted them, cracking a joke with one and teasing another. The laughter and confusion prevented even a closing prayer. This invasion marked a turning point, for the meeting thereafter became more informal, even casual, with babies howling and young children playing on the floor.

One of the women he helped was Gwen Levitt. "I'd like to meet your husband," he told her and turned up at her home one cold evening and helped himself to a slice of apple tart. Jim admitted that he had not read the Bible since his school days. "We'll look at it together one of these days," said George. "What about coming round to the club tonight for a game of snooker after the boys have gone home?" Jim came at eleven p.m. and some years later he joined Skipper's Christian 'Searching Group' leading on to confirmation classes.

George also became friendly with Jim's brother Ted who as owner of a driving school, betting shops and greyhounds reckoned he knew most rackets going. "I always thought church people had to be a hundred per cent," Ted argued, but George corrected him. After hearing George's list of misdemeanours Ted considered that he himself was not such a bad fellow after all. Yet he could never make George out. "Is he a confidence trickster?" he wondered. Nevertheless he accepted the Bible George presented to him and read it.

The Halseys welcomed George into their home as one of the family. He met Jenny through visiting the wives' meeting. A short, vivacious blonde, Jenny had three young children and a husband whom George longed to tackle. One day he saw Bob in the street washing his car. "Why not come over and use our hose pipe?" George invited him. Bob stayed for a cup of tea and was intrigued by George's down to earth reasoning about the existence of a Creator.

Some of George's contacts with adults were forged through visiting the teenagers' parents, and he became involved with financial problems, matrimonial disputes and religious parleys in his efforts to win them. By the time Skipper returned from Australia there were more than a dozen newly converted adults who looked to George as their spiritual father. He needed their loyalty, for he anticipated a clash between adults and teenagers. "The more I hear, 'the young people must mix with the adults' the more I realise the ridiculousness of it and see that the old people must mix with the young people. They were young once. Teenagers haven't been old yet."

Although he shielded his teenage converts from adult interference George believed that it was necessary to hold social events for all members of the family. On Family Nights the club room and canteen were thrown open for games, singing and a get-together for all except the tiny children who were cared for in the nursery school. The Christians began to introduce their neighbours and friends to these functions as a first step to asking them to church.

After Skipper's return the staff decided to run an outing for church members and their families on some Sundays after the morning Communion service. George commandeered every available car to supplement the Centre's two coaches. One memorable Sunday the whole Mayflower church family drove to a quiet corner of Epping Forest and took part in an open air Communion Service. A picnic and an afternoon spent together deepened relationships within the growing Christian family.

By the summer of 1964 George was leading back to Blankenburge a party of ten family groups which included David and Grace Sheppard with two year old Jenny. The decaying hotel had been ideal for the teenage parties of previous years, but the broken chairs and dusty bedrooms shocked some of the adults. First impressions, however, were soon forgotten under the genius of George's leadership. "Skipper, I want you to have one of the worst rooms," George said. "If you and Grace can stick that poky back one, then no one else will be able to complain." The Sheppards stoically accepted the viewless room, sagging bed, and precarious wash-basin.

George's bedroom, the biggest in the hotel, became the group's meeting-place. An oil cooker and kettle made cups of tea possible at any time of day or night. He invited different people in to speak to them about Christ. After several talks with Sheila she committed herself to Christ. Her husband Rich preferred to wait until he returned to the cold reality of daily work in the docks before making his decision.

For their last evening George instigated an entertainment, and smiled contentedly as he watched the quiet ones unfold in the family circle. Out of the camaraderie 'The 64 Group' was formed back in Canning Town to produce another more ambitious entertainment one Saturday night.

"Can we go away together again?" some of 'The 64 Group' asked George. But he now foresaw the danger of an exclusive clique. "I'll run a weekend for *all* the church members next Easter," was his answer. In due course a fleet of buses and cars transported a hundred adults, teenagers and toddlers to Ashburnham. There in the stately home, surrounded by stables, outhouses, lakes and woods the Mayflower family spent Easter. The adults slept in the imposing dormitories giggling at memories of their camping days. George encouraged pillow fights, but a flooded bathroom made him bark his disapproval at the culprits.

While the weekend bound everyone together it also exposed once again the difference in outlook between adults and teenagers. Before leaving George summoned everyone to help clear up. Ted Lyons senior was infuriated to find some boys, his own son among them, sprawled across the beds he had been detailed to move to another room. "It's not right that we should have to clear their room. They should do it themselves," he protested to George.

George was by now at the height of his power and wielded authority in every sphere. Other staff, residents, local adults and teenagers looked for his sanction, on which the execution of every idea depended. From his arm chair George Burton's personality permeated the Centre and beyond, so that even ex-residents could not help asking themselves apprehensively, "Would Mr. Burton approve of this?" While still giving close allegiance to skipper, he carved out for himself the position of controlling all decisions.

Despite his pre-occupation with large numbers George adhered to his basic belief that souls were won through personal work in homes. For several years the Sheppards used their home to attract others through small informal meetings, working in partnership with a young couple, Colin and Mary Watts. The team of workers gradually increased, but the work was slow and often discouraging. While Skipper was in Australia the few couples concerned asked permission to have a 'fish and chip supper' at the Mayflower. It was a success, but George was uneasy, as he reported to Skipper.

"Now people have got ideas about using the club premises and I feel very strongly that this should not happen. The usual showing of films and social evenings is not having effect in the majority of churches in Britain and you found your stupid men's club was not a success and started to concentrate on homes. Skipper, keep away from numbers. Please see that half a dozen in the close intimacy of a home talking about Christian things is far better than fifty or sixty people watching a Christian film. It might not look so impressive but I believe that the vision that God gave you to use homes is the best way."

George was relieved at Skipper's reply. "Something is always trying to lead us back to the institutional church, rather than the small, living groups."

At a weekend conference held soon after this for all the voluntary helpers, George clarified the aim: "You can put on a lot of things and you'll get people to come. We could have rock and roll for the teenagers one night and old time dancing for the adults another night. But is it right to put on these things just because we've got the premises? We run things to win souls for Christ."

In the autumn of 1963 George and the staff planned a meal in his flat for all the church couples who might be willing to open their homes to bring the gospel to their neighbours through informal meetings. The staff realised that local leaders would only be developed if the men in each home chaired these meetings instead of relying on Skipper or a staff member. This gathering of some fifteen couples was a landmark.

CHAPTER 10

Senior Leaders

"Where there is no vision the people perish" (Proverbs twenty-nine, verse eighteen) George took as his motto. His 'vision' was to train local Christians to lead the youth work and other departments. Although he was prepared to use some adults, his main source of supply was the Sunday Group, for he reckoned that those who had experienced the freedom of his flat would be more likely to reproduce similar groups when they established their own homes.

The various groups in operation were providing a training ground for his first leaders, Jim and Bill, Len and his fiancée Pat, and Rita; then Rita's fiancé Alan, Jill and Ted. By the end of 1963 there were twenty, now called Senior Leaders to distinguish them from younger members of the Sunday Group who were also helping to run the groups. A year later the number had reached twenty-seven.

George expected many to fall away, but dreaded the gibes which might then be levelled at him. "Will Skipper still want me, or will he give me the push?" he fretted. He itched to quit and open his own work in a little mission hall or return to the Arab world.

He was worried too about his health. His doctor kept urging him to diet, and then delivered an ultimatum, "If you don't knock off a few stone, I give you two years to live." Burdened by surplus weight he was always panting by the time he had climbed the stairs. Moments of anxiety spurred him to diet for a meal or two, but he could not curb his passion for toast, jam and creamy cakes, and his weight remained over fifteen stone.

Pining to leave, he knew he was called to be with the young leaders; longing to succeed, he was scared of failure; aching to be independent, he was flung back on the support of others. He was trapped. Yet if he relented, his leaders would drift. So he whipped himself on to nurture them. When they were absent he found out why. If the reason was sickness, he visited; if relationships were strained he ironed out the quarrel and coaxed them back. In even the most unpromising material he discerned the seed of leadership and set about cultivating it. One whose first taste of responsibility was to stand on duty by the swimming-bath swelled with pride when George congratulated him.

He studied the methods of Jesus Christ with His disciples. Did He not spend a disproportionate amount of time with just twelve? And after three years they were filled with the Holy Spirit and turned the world upside down. George prayed that these young people too would learn to be guided by the Holy Spirit rather than by books and education.

He was unyielding in his determination that they should not ape middle-class patterns of behaviour as if these were essential to Christian growth. They had to stay natural, unaffected and in touch with their families and friends with a view to winning them. He considered that in time Christ Himself would mould them, though he was quick to guide their thinking as well. Once he noticed some of his Senior Leaders laughing at the contents of a paper. Snatching it from them he saw the subject was pornographic and began to read it aloud. "Anyone can make up this stuff if it's in their minds," he declared. "Who wants to keep it?" He offered the paper to each in turn. "I've never read that sort of thing," one parried. "Rita wouldn't let me take it home," said Alan. "Tear it up," suggested another, and they all agreed. "It's like looking a girl up and down," he told them. "You can't help catching sight of an attractive girl and wanting her, but you don't have to keep staring at her. You can turn away."

"Prayer is talking to God," he pointed out, "anywhere and at any time." He tried to be with new converts as they uttered their first audible prayers. While he did not believe in introducing them too soon to formal prayer meetings which were often dominated by a few adults, he did gather his leaders to pray together and rejoiced at their spontaneous praises. "Thank you, Lord, that you have sent us people who understand us," prayed Len. And Jim added, "Thank you that Mrs. Olley don't shush us in church no more."

Of the many weekends away it was not until June 1963 that George attempted to organise a Bible teaching weekend and he told Skipper about it.

"We went down on Friday night and after some tea they went to their rooms and pillow fought until the early hours of the morning. There was laughter and screams with records blaring away until after one a.m. They came for breakfast when they wanted.

"For the first time in my life I prepared a Bible exhibition and if I may say so humbly it was good.

"I did not start my first session until five o'clock on Saturday so they were absolutely free to explore the place before we got down to why we were there. But they also had time to see the exhibition at their leisure and practically everyone came and asked Jean and I questions. So we were able to deal with people individually. On the Sunday afternoon we had a question time and it was really wonderful."

The letter ended typically:

"I am afraid that I have blotted my copy book at Mabledon for we broke four windows and did one or two more bits of damage. Fortunately some Christians staying there had a collection on the Sunday morning which came to £7 11s and they gave it to me towards repair of broken windows."

Jim was keen to do serious Bible study ahead of the others and George promoted him to lead the Sunday Group Bible studies. He lent him books which he had freshly read himself. Then he suggested that Jim, Len and later Ted should study to become lay readers. When he saw the syllabus his courage nearly failed, for he wondered how they would ever manage it. "I can't see how all this study is going to help you preach Christ any better," he growled. "But I suppose you have got to fit in with these stupid rules of the Church of England." He toyed with the thought of doing the course himself and becoming their tutor, but other commitments forced him to relinquish his protégés to Skipper's care. Nevertheless his pride was unconcealed when Jim passed the New Testament paper.

One Sunday evening Jim and Len preached in the chapel. Len raised all his old objections to Christianity and Jim tried to meet them. Another time the Senior Leaders prepared and led an evening service by themselves.

11

George jealously guarded his young leaders from the diverting influence of other Christians. Once a missionary came and George asked Jim to show him round the clubs. Then George suddenly remembered he had meant to warn the visitor not to entice Jim to join his work in France. He dashed off, and drew the missionary to one side out of Jim's hearing. He was too late: the request had already been made. George was boiling and ordered him to withdraw his words. "I can't trust anyone to leave my young people alone," he stormed. "We'll never get a work established here if they all go off abroad, or go to train at colleges."

An exception to his rule was Dr. A. T. Schofield whom George invited to speak about Uganda. Jim asked him afterwards, "Would you say it is easier to witness as a Christian abroad than in your own country?" "Yes," replied Dr. Schofield, "we draw back from speaking to the chap at the next bench. It is easier to go and shout on the street corner of a strange town." Jim had extracted the point in true Burton style and added, "I wanted to get that one straight because many people think they must go abroad to the wilds to be missionaries." Jim's closing prayer summed up George's longings. "Thank you, Lord, for sending missionaries out to Africa and other places. But England is a mission field and there is much to be done here. There are many thousands dying each day who have no knowledge of Yourself. Lord, we pray that the Christians in Britain can stay and tell others at work, in the office, on the street, of Yourself."

George seldom pushed his young people to large meetings. "They'll go when they're strong enough not to be put off," he pronounced. Late in 1965 some of the Senior Leaders attended an East London convention. They returned in high spirits bursting to tell their leader about it. "Let's have some tea and toast upstairs," he suggested and asked Skipper to join them. He ordered a resident to bring the food up to his flat immediately. He guffawed as they described to him the tedious opening prayer full of Thees and Thous and unintelligible expressions. Afterwards Ted expressed the concern of them all when he prayed, "Lord, may we never lose the common touch."

George was glad for his leaders to gain experience in speaking at other churches, though he stipulated that all invitations were to be made through him alone and slated anyone who failed to comply.

He was careful to forestall jealousy among them and knew the right time to promote one and hold back another. At first he sent them in twos or threes to prevent them exaggerating their testimonies and so that they could report on each other's performances when they returned.

The Judo Group, trained by Len, became a team of witness. They visited various churches and after their demonstration spoke about their faith. "Why do we come here and do judo?" Len put to their hosts. "Not just for a laugh. We do it so that we can tell you about Christ."

But there were also less successful evenings as their diary tells.

"There were about thirty young people and there was no one who seemed able to get them quiet and different ones kept chipping in. They were not very interested except when Ray hit his head on the edge of a mat. Len also got kicked in the back, and Sylvie felt sick on the way home."

However, another church was so impressed that the vicar invited them to join a house-party for his youth group. Ted's message was, "Christianity isn't just rules. Christianity is Christ, following Christ, and He leads us in different ways." A West Indian boy remarked to them, "I've never heard anyone talk about Christianity as you lot do. Everyone try and give you some rules that you must carry out, and every time you break those rules you're a backslider."

Bill was once struggling to make himself heard above some noisy troublemakers at a North London youth club. "It's wonderful to see you joking and answering back even while I am talking. You've got some go, some life. What about giving that life to Christ and using it in His service?"

Apart from prayer, Bible study and speaking engagements the Senior Leaders were kept busy running the groups of younger teenagers. While boosting their confidence in public, George prevented undue conceit by brutally frank assessments in private. Jim especially received harsh treatment as George curbed his natural urge for ascendancy.

After the initial interest the group leaders' meetings, held in the Ops Room, flagged and for nine months not a single meeting was held. George had other pressures and he hesitated to allow Jim to call one on his own initiative. It was not until June 1964 that he let Jim chair a meeting, and then he made a point of wandering in to show them he was still in charge. "This is what I've worked and prayed for," he commented feelingly, "but it's hard for me to see you growing up and not needing me any more."

The Senior Leaders worked hard, but George knew just when to lay on an outing to lift morale. Their first one was to Southend where they had a slap-up lunch and a train trip to the end of the pier. Later that summer he toured North Italy with seven of them. "I've got to give time to these few," he resolved. He hired a red minibus and arranged for Jim to drive for most of the trip while he sat beside him, talking, 'sowing seeds', grooming him.

Florence was their base and there they sucked at spaghetti strings, swam in the Arno and danced at a night club. In Venice George haggled with some gondoliers who gave them a cut-price trip round the canals. Ted's birthday provided the excuse for a gay dinner party at the water's edge. George spent the afternoon looking for a suitable restaurant and negotiating reasonable terms. On the Sunday they held their own service at which Jim preached. Len introduced him as "Mr. Jim Gosling, B.D.", which Jim interpreted appropriately as "Burton's Diploma".

The following year George again concentrated on the leaders in planning a holiday to Germany, and to save expense he ambitiously decided to travel in the Centre's old coach, overhauled and repainted for the occasion. Inside he had a special cupboard fitted for stores of food and a cabinet for serving tea along the way. Ted painted a Union Jack at the rear and the sign 'Right Hand Drive' in three languages. Before going, a few set-backs caused George a sleepless night; but then he remembered the Bible's advice, "Cast all your care upon Him, for He careth for you." The next day he could affirm, "He is completely in control."

The sixteen young people and four adults started off light-heartedly with George at the wheel. But fifty miles along the Ostend–Brussels motorway disaster struck. A smell of burning made George pull in. Steam was spurting from the leaking radiator which cracked irreparably as someone poured water into it. Calling everyone together George led them in prayer at the roadside. He ordered them to clear their luggage out of the coach and wait while he and Jean hitched a lift to Brussels. There he tracked down the biggest Bedford dealer in the city and learnt that the position was hopeless, as all the garages were on a week's national holiday. However his sad story was so cogently told that the manager and three colleagues were soon on their way in the firm's limousines to rescue the stranded English holiday-makers and take them in style to the railway station, while a breakdown lorry towed the coach to their workshop for repairs.

At Frieburg they had to eat out instead of providing meals from their stores; and as they were feeling the pinch they made their finances a matter for prayer. A prompt answer came when a local minister first invited them to a social evening and a meal and then saved further expense by ferrying their luggage to the station. But the group most clearly saw God working out His purpose on their boat trip down the Rhine. They met a party of Americans and by the time they got off at Cöblenz George had led one of them to Christ.

The 'special treatment' lavished on the Senior Leaders sparked off some jealousy among the rest of the Sunday Group. During a week-end away one of the Maintenance Group expressed his antagonism by smearing Jim's bed with jam. In order to cool down the heated atmosphere George cracked a joke. "Arthur, you're coming on, you know. Some time ago you wouldn't have admitted you had done it. You would have said someone else done it!" The Group laughed and George went on, "I've allowed quite a few of you to come up and I have not been around myself, with the result that a number have not been prepared to accept orders. If the Senior Leaders give you a reasonable order you are going to obey it. If you don't, don't come up into my flat. Simple language."

Then Pat Howell diplomatically took some of the blame for the rift between the Senior Leaders and the rest of the Group. "I was shocked when somebody says to me the other day, 'Oh, we thought you were stuck up!' I realise now that I have not been talking to the younger members. I think we've all got to try to mix more." George closed the session by proposing, "Let's put some jam on Arthur's head. It will make your hair grow, Arthur!"

George strove to establish Christian homes in Canning Town and abetted romances between Group members. One courting couple had a stormy row. "Sit down and I'll get a cup of tea," he consoled Pat who was moping and longing for a reconciliation. While the kettle was boiling he went for Len. "Come and have a cup of tea with me," he said, and strolled back with him to the kitchen. "Oh, can I introduce you two?" he laughed as they caught sight of each other.

Len and Pat were married in June 1964 and used to invite other young people to their home, until they emigrated to Canada. Despite his disappointment George accepted their departure as God's will for them and did not attempt to dissuade them.

Alan and Rita had several problems and spent hours talking things over with George. When he offered to assist with their wedding arrangements they gladly accepted. He organised a score of people to make refreshments and prepare the club room for the reception. He even drove them to the train for their honeymoon, for he felt as if they were his own children.

Noticing all this Jim and Janet decided to make their own wedding plans without consulting Mr. Burton. They booked the Town Hall, a professional caterer and a date in Skipper's diary before Jim eventually asked if he could recommend a hotel in the Isle of Wight. Although he felt snubbed George now offered to take over their reception arrangements. They declined and George retired to spend a sleepless night with a huge 'Do Not Disturb' notice displayed on his door. Jim came to see him the next day and George sobbed, "I know you're growing up, Jim, and you must make your own arrangements. I've got to accept that you don't need me now."

He might not have been needed for wedding arrangements, but he was needed for accommodation. "If we are going to keep these young couples in the area we must provide flats for them," George had foreseen as early as 1961. With Skipper he conceived the idea of forming a housing association to acquire property locally. Once he was in a cinema when he suddenly obeyed an impulse to carry on his hard search. An agent's notice led him to 78, Stopford Road, an attractive house that could easily be converted into three separate living units, and it was soon bought for the Mayflower Housing Association.

George assumed a large part of the management of the house, which became a constant headache to him. "We must leave the flats empty rather than get the wrong tenants in," he decreed as he drew up a list of every possible applicant. The staff were strongly aware of the danger of breeding 'rice-Christians'. So among the criteria they laid down was that both partners should have proved themselves as Christians and that they should be regular church members and actively involved in work at the Mayflower.

The first tenants included Alan and Rita, Dennis and Jim and Janet Gosling. Within two years the Mayflower Housing Association bought three more houses, and George's prayers were realised as other Senior Leaders set up their homes in Canning Town.

CHAPTER 11

The Book

"Fatty Burton, Fatty Burton," yelled Ted Lyons as he ran on to the stage. "You're yeller, Ted," shouted an imitation of George's voice. Jim Gosling appeared, puffing in exaggerated Burton style. He was dressed in George's baggy blue pullover stuffed with a cushion, and the sight of him set the audience rocking with laughter. George himself, sitting in the front row with Helena, choked and spluttered with mirth as the Sunday Group members enacted scenes of the past five years. The Mayflower's theatre was packed with a crowd of well-wishers for a party held in May 1965 to celebrate the publication of George's book, *People Matter More than Things*.

Ted Lyons was reliving his first days in the club when he and his mates bawled insults at George from outside during the chapel services. Afterwards George would chat with them in the street. Other scenes traced Ted's journey from doubt to faith in Christ and culminated in his presenting to George a five foot high canvas portraying Christ with Doubting Thomas. On the back Ted had written, 'Presented to Mr. George Burton because he brought me to God through the Lord Jesus Christ. May God make him happy always.'

Then Ted's mother stood up to read her poem.

"We have all come here this evening, just to say,
  How happy we all are, your book is on its way,
  To you it must seem, you're sending a friend
  Out on a journey that need never end.
  You're trying to explain, trying to help people understand
  Situations and teenagers who get out of hand.
  If only they who don't agree could be here tonight to look
    around and see
  So many faces, they would think 'I wish that I were he
  Whom Jesus Christ had inspired to write this book' . . .

We haven't brought you a present, Mr. Burton, or anything,
Just ourselves, 'cause to you, *People Matter More than Things*."

In seconding the toast to George and his book, Jean had paid her
tribute. "I have been closely associated with George Burton in the
work here right from its start. It is not easy to be harnessed to a
stick of dynamite, but if it contains the power to move mountains,
then I'd rather be there than sitting beside a harmless sparkler."
As the party drew to a close, David Sheppard rose to speak.

"I wonder how many of you who know Mr. Burton well have
sometimes been made to think of St. Paul? He says, 'I'm worse
than all the other apostles. I'm not fit to be called an apostle.
However it's by God's grace that I am what I am. In my labours
I have outdone them all—not I indeed, but the grace of God
working with me!' Yes, Paul wasn't afraid to say, 'God has
worked mightily through me'. Yet when you got close to Paul, it
wasn't boasting. We thank God very much, all of us, for what
George's friendship has meant to us and I am proud to call him
my friend."

As he watched and listened, George thanked the One who had
answered his childish prayer repeated throughout his wilderness
years, "God help me to help humanity, especially the poor boys, and
help me with my reading and writing." It was God who had enabled
him to produce a book.

His share of the writing had been done during the fortnight in
Switzerland two years earlier when he had feverishly copied out the
full notes which he had asked David Hewitt to write. Months previously George had dictated pages of headings and told David to
write all he could about them. "I believe other people could learn
from me," he said, "and I want to get some of this stuff on to paper."
He had not yet entrusted David with the secret of his writing
phobia and David had no reason to suspect it.
From Switzerland George wrote excitedly to Jean, "I have
written so far 139 foolscap pages about youth work and I know that
I have another 100 sheets to come out of me. Personally I think
some of it is very good and now I realise that one just doesn't sit

down and write a book off the cuff. I wish you were nearer so as I could talk to you about it for I am scared of tearing it up. If I sent it to the bank and asked them to keep it that would probably be the end of it for at least another ten years. I thank God that He has given me the power over the pen."

The sight of pages of his own handwriting filled him with a mixture of pride and panic. The only other writing of any length he had ever accomplished was his outline autobiography written during his holiday in Majorca. He had it typed, but the original manuscript terrified him so much that in a fit of hysteria he had ripped it to pieces and stuffed it into the boiler.

Six months after his return from Switzerland George unearthed the embryo of his book on youth work. An ordinand, Ian Elliott, had taken David Hewitt's place and when George discovered that he could type he committed it to him to work on. It ran without headings or punctuation, so Ian's task was to divide it into chapters.

There were still gaps in the story's sequence and in an effort to help George fill them, Jean and Ian compiled some points for further expansion. George went off with Ian and a tape-recorder, and Ian 'interviewed' him, trying to draw him out to express his ideas. The effort failed miserably, for George quite untypically froze to the point of paralysis. Eager to transfer his ideas on to paper, but unable to write or even speak them, what could he do? He resorted to persuading others to answer the questions for him and the material thus collected was inserted in the appropriate chapters.

As Skipper, Jean and Ian studied the typescript he forbade any two of them to work without the third, for fear they should criticise him. At first he insisted that they should refer every alteration to him, until the process became too painful. They suggested adding material to give the book sequence and shape, and Jean offered to formulate it and then to write the opening chapter as well. He liked it and, to make it 'his own', drafted the opening paragraphs and read the rest on to a tape recorder.

The book was filling out and George wondered how he could have it published. He considered having it duplicated but Skipper encouraged him to fly higher. At the party to celebrate publication of his own autobiography, *Parson's Pitch*, he mentioned George's manuscript to his publishers' representative. "Send us what you've written as soon as you can," came the reply, and eight chapters reached them within a week. Back came an enthusiastic report from their reader. "A valuable book for its understanding of the difference between working-class and middle-class outlook and its insistence that conversion means conversion to Christ and not to middle-class culture; for the author's understanding of the kind of teenagers who present the most challenging and rewarding sphere of work for the club leader; and for the heartening stories of successful evangelism. The book appeals to me strongly as a convincing account of an exacting enterprise, which should serve to guide and encourage Christian youth workers generally."

George read and re-read the report, hardly believing his eyes. He had copies typed and passed them round. So his book would be published after all. How soon could he let them have the finished manuscript? It still needed a final chapter which he asked Jean to write. As a post-script he decided to add a chapter showing the steps towards salvation. He requested several people to write the chapter for him and sent the product to David Hewitt, then at theological college.

"Please titlivate [*sic*] this for me and return the draft as soon as possible," he urged. "Don't show it round to the others for I want them to buy a copy themselves. I am asking my friends to pray particularly for Chapter ten, 'How can I accept Christ?' It is exciting that it is going to be on hundreds of non-Christian bookstalls."

It was a strangely subdued George who donned his best suit and unaccustomed tie to go and fix terms with the publishers. The book was to be a five shilling paperback. Printing would take about nine months and they would need a short outline of the author's life on the back cover. Tears of emotion trickled down as he signed the contract.

His mood of awe progressed to one of apprehension. What would people, especially Canning Town people, think of his book? He had carefully included some reference to each of his Senior Leaders, for he knew they would all be expecting one. He got a typist to list all the sixty people mentioned and made a point of seeing each one to gain their assent.

"What about other youth leaders?" he flinched. "They won't

agree with a lot of what I've written." He asked Jean to examine points likely to be picked on. The vulnerable spots including his condoning of immoral behaviour, his lack of post-conversion teaching, and his over-protection of converts. He sent the possible criticisms to David Hewitt with a note, "Answer these for me, David. You know what I would say."

George himself spent hours thrashing out his replies to unseen critics. "This is how *we* have been led to act here in Canning Town," he argued. "These methods aren't necessarily applicable to other areas. But I still think that middle-class Christians will have a lot to learn from all this."

"Have you any ideas for publicising the book?" the publishers inquired. Ideas? George bristled with them. "Get some bookmarkers printed, say 5,000. We can send them to all readers of the Mayflower *Log*. Then I want some large posters. I've got volunteers who will display them as sandwich-men in the City to catch the business people." George was not finished. "We have a couple of coaches, and we can plaster them with posters and drive them round London full of Canning Town kids. They'd love it! They could get out at different places like Trafalgar Square or the Embankment and tell everyone they meet about the book." Jean thought she was hardened by now, but she felt herself blushing.

For the first time in his life George dared to contact past acquaintances. He was an author now, and they would be proud to have known him. He issued a letter to everyone he could think of, enclosing a bookmarker which they were expected to pass on. He planned a party to celebrate the publication and invited all his old St. Paul's friends. Madame Tullio from his restaurant days was one person he specially wanted to be present. He would invite Eva and her husband, for without her help he might never have ventured to think of writing a book.

In November 1964 he wrote to David Hewitt, "Hodders have just written to say they can't bring my book out before August. I have really prayed hard that the Lord would bring it out in the month of May." By the New Year he was informed that publication date was fixed for May 10th.

George fingered proudly the advance copies and admired his photograph on the glossy red cover. He sent an autographed copy to some two hundred youth leaders, probation officers, magistrates, builders, scaffolders and sports outfitters who had supplied the Mayflower with equipment or helped in other ways. He carried a copy in his pocket wherever he went and introduced his book as a talking point with complete strangers. He toured the Christian bookshops making himself known to managers and salesgirls alike. "They'll have a personal interest now," he explained.

Visitors to the Mayflower were confronted not only with striking posters, but also with the author himself. They could hardly resist buying a copy after hearing George's propaganda. "There's a very good book out at the moment—the best I have ever read. There's a picture on the back of the fellow who wrote it. It's called *People Matter More than Things*, and it will cost you five bob. I want to see the book used to win souls. Read it. Pass it on to others."

Even so, George was taken aback at the book's success. A month after publication a further 5,000 copies were printed, and a second reprint by the end of the year. In July it became a best seller among religious paperbacks. The critics greeted it as 'an exhilarating account'. Most reviewers held reservations about George's methods, but as one put it, "this man gets to the people who need the gospel, by a wise and patient policy of 'sitting where they sit' ". "George Burton is an uncomfortable companion," wrote a Church Army reviewer. "I don't like this book, but if it leads us to our knees, helps us to face reality, and accept a greater measure of sacrifice, it will have done its job." *The Franciscan* was favourable; but it was Dr. William Barclay in the *Expository Times* who pleased George most. Picking out various incidents described in the book he asked, "Is George Burton right? Say what you like, he has done a magnificent job. He has got much to teach every youth leader."

CHAPTER 12

Widening Circles

"Lord, put me in the pulpit so that I may preach for you," George prayed one day. The next morning Skipper, too ill to move from bed, sent for George to take his place that afternoon and preach at the service which ended the Mayflower garden party. This surely was God's answer and George readily agreed. He rehearsed his sermon painstakingly and recorded it on tape lest he should panic; and for good measure he had a message from Skipper taped as well. In the pulpit, however, his nervousness vanished, for he was inspired by the sight of a little girl smiling up at him. With vigorous fluency he exhorted his hearers to receive Jesus Christ into their lives.

After that he preached only rarely. "What is the Bible?" he posed at one evening service. "It is sixty-six books divided into the Old Testament and the New Testament, but it is all about Christ. Things were written about Christ years before He was ever born. Isn't it thrilling? I've only just recently found it out for myself and I want to share it with you. It's knowing the Author of the book that counts, not the book itself. If you know Him you will have eternal life. If you don't," and his voice rose to a crescendo, "no matter who you are, you are going to hell!"

For the first few years George could seldom be lured outside the Mayflower to speak about the work, and he disliked the other staff members going either. "We've got to get something started here before we can speak about it," he insisted. In June 1961 he did however address a mission team of undergraduates at St. Aldate's Church, Oxford. "A missionary," he told them, "is someone who tells other people about Jesus Christ. As you go knocking on doors you will get nervous, for the devil, who is the prince of this world, will try and upset you. As soon as you get talking about Christ it will be a battle, for the devil puts in all his forces. You will perhaps be called away to a meal. I say to you, go without your meal and continue to talk about Christ."

Later as people heard of his success in training local leaders, and particularly after the publication of his book, George received invitations to speak at churches and colleges. In a Cambridge college he got so engrossed in conversation that he had to leave by clambering over the railings after midnight. The first theological college to invite him in June 1963 was the London College of Divinity. In trepidation at the prospect he sent David Hewitt away to prepare an outline.

Once on his feet he held his audience. "I was told this was your pastoralia hour," he started. "I looked the word up in my dictionary but couldn't find it." The students applauded his frankness. "I've been asked to speak on the Principles and Problems of the Open Youth Club, with suggestions of how the problems can be met. Well, there's only one principle: winning souls for the Lord Jesus Christ. Your problem: Satan. A suggestion for how to meet him: by prayer, trusting in the power of the Holy Spirit."

He enlarged on his introduction. "This is what happens to you curates. You say, 'Well, I had better fit in with what happened before.' If you dare to do something different you can be sure that someone will tell you, 'That's not how our previous curate did it'. Try to educate your vicar. Some of them have got into a rut. You must be loyal to your vicar, but that doesn't mean to your vicar's wife! I'm asking some of you to think of opening the doors to young people outside the church. You will be told by the church council, 'We tried it once and a couple of windows were broken.' Well I wouldn't like to stand in front of the Lord Jesus one day and say that I forbade the gospel message being preached because someone broke a window. I'm asking you to open your club to boys and girls. Give them time, love and understanding. Put people before things."

In full flow George crammed the next hour with the fruit of his experience at the Mayflower and the students rose to cheer him out. In time he spoke at other theological colleges ending with Oakhill College, Southgate, where he was in a bad mood and sensed hostility. "You should have asked me here before," he began. "I haven't prepared anything, so you'd better ask questions. Who's the Senior Student? I'm sure you've got one prepared." It was a tricky one, and he swung it over to Jean who had been brought to lend moral support. No sooner had she started than he broke in. Then he carried on, answering questions and telling what God had done through him at the Mayflower. Urging them to go out and win souls, he confessed, "For years I attended prayer meetings and prayed for souls, but I never told anyone about Jesus. I hope you lot aren't going to think little prayer meetings are enough. You've got to get into homes and win souls individually."

His hardest ordeal was in facing the Frontier Youth Trust Conference of youth leaders in April 1965. Recalling his clashes with some of them a few years previously, he quailed at their anticipated criticisms of his talk on Home Grown Leaders. He could only tackle the assignment by answering questions prepared for him by Skipper. He harangued them as Christian youth leaders to remember their calling to win souls, but he was touchy and at a later session flared up at an imagined rebuke from the chairman. "I've made a fool of myself," he admitted ruefully. "What will they think of me now?"

The inmates of Wandsworth Prison were an easier audience and enjoyed his visits. He took a table tennis team and, guessing that the men would desire most of all to see a pair of female legs, always included some girls. At a detention centre he gained an immediate response from seventy teenagers by taking off his jacket, loosening his tie and cracking a quick joke or two.

When the B.B.C. were presenting David Sheppard on the television programme 'This is Your Life', George was enrolled to make his derogatory speech about cricket. At the rehearsal he heard that Sheppard's conversion was diluted to a 'decision to enter the Church', and George himself was supposed to say that Skipper aimed merely to turn the club members into better citizens. He revealed nothing of his intentions, but as the camera focused on him George left his nation-wide audience in no doubt that Skipper's aim was to lead the Canning Town boys to a faith in the Lord Jesus Christ.

With the work gathering momentum it became convenient for the staff to set aside an evening every month or two when visitors could inspect the Centre. George was lavish and pressing in inviting to these 'at homes' acquaintances made in shops or while nosing out club equipment. The party of up to fifty guests would be divided into two for the tour. "I know you all want to go with the Reverend David Sheppard," he read the minds of his group, "but some of you have got to come with me. Anyway I'll tell you more about the work than he will." He made sure that none left without hearing the way of salvation. Many were offended by his rude manner which contrasted so strikingly with Sheppard's.

Sometimes the Christian Union from a London college or hospital would offer to come and spend a day working at the Mayflower. George took delight in organising these visits to the minutest detail, and from his accumulated experience of such parties he produced a memorandum on the subject. His key maxim was "Check, check, and re-check." Every year a party of society young ladies came from the House of Citizenship and his vociferous vending of Christianity held them spellbound. Never had they met anyone like George Burton.

Once a youth chaplain asked to bring two or three hundred people to visit the Centre. "I'd love to take over," George volunteered, and mobilised all residents to absorb the invasion. His arrangements for hospitality, a film, touring the premises, talking to them and laying on a trampoline demonstration ensured a memorable afternoon.

Dog-collared clergy nettled him, for he both envied their status and despised them for being out of touch with ordinary people. They provided a target for his aggression and many went away scandalised from their encounter with him. "Do you think I hit the collar too hard?" he once asked Jean. "Yes, sometimes." "Well, I believe I am *called* to hit it," he claimed vehemently.

If a mere dog-collar produced such reactions, an Archbishop was sure to be inflammable material. When Dr. and Mrs. Coggan came, George arranged for his Senior Leaders to meet them in his flat. Paradoxically, he had often prompted Len to think of entering the ordained ministry, but the qualifications required were too steep. Pat, Len's wife, asked the Archbishop if he thought it should be made easier for working-class people to 'enter the church'. Dr. Coggan corrected her, "You mean, 'be ordained'." George interpreted this as revealing his own as well as Pat's lack of education and snapped at him, "You know perfectly well what she means!" Fortunately the Archbishop redeemed himself later. "Does God promise us peace?" he was asked. Unhesitatingly came the reply, "Yes—and war."

George stressed that visitors should not expect special treatment but fit in with what was going on. An elderly lady who winced at the deafening twangs of a practising guitar group was told to get out in the garden if she could not endure the din. A visitor to the hostel complained that the racket from the teenagers disturbed her baby. "Your baby will have to take the noise. I'm not stopping the teenagers," George informed her.

If George showed up worst with people he feared would expose his poor education, he was at his best with those whom others overlooked or ignored. When a Christian couple turned up two hours early for a garden party, George ushered them in for a meal and made them feel needed by giving them a job on a stall. Afterwards he saw his new friends to the door, gripping them warmly by the hand and kissing the old lady on her cheek.

Many casual callers knocked at the Centre's doors. George never gave money and berated a well-meaning resident who once did so. "Are you prepared to follow that man through?" he demanded. "Who's going to give him money when he comes again?" If George would not give money, yet many a stranger went on his way feeling that at least someone cared. One evening George listened to the story of a homeless woman over a cup of tea. "God answers all our prayers with 'Yes', 'No' or 'Wait'," he explained to her and then prayed that God would provide for her family. Some months later he received a letter from her: "I know that this cottage is the answer to your very sincere prayers said for a family you never even knew."

With the publication of his book George's correspondence multiplied. He never hesitated to commandeer the services of someone to sit while he dictated. He had acquired a managerial roll-top desk, but he hardly ever sat at it. Instead he signed his correspondence from his huge arm-chair over a tiny table on castors which was always littered with papers. "Doesn't it look impressive?" he congratulated himself as he surveyed the room with its newly-erected book shelves. "Do you believe me when I tell you that I never used to read or write?" he asked Jean countless times.

George diligently acknowledged every gift of material and equipment. When necessary he reminded Skipper also to write. "People want your signature, Skipper. God has given you a name to use for Him."

Letters meant much to George and he hoarded them all. "They prove to me that somebody wants and needs me." A number of people wrote about the effect of his book. He was moved by a tribute from an old 'fellow pilgrim in her ninety-third year'. "It has given me much valuable guidance in my life here in this Old Age Home. I have often been afraid of witnessing to others for the Lord and you have helped me over this stile. Thank you."

Despite the diversion of his book, the work still had to go on. A new sense of urgency seized him as difficulty with breathing made him concerned about his health. "I'm scared of the future: I don't want to be put out to grass when Skipper doesn't need me." "You won't ever retire, George," Jean forecast. "You'll die in harness."

Where could he go after the Mayflower? His relationship with Helena was as good as it had ever been since their separation, and she came to him at the Centre every week. She, however, had her bed-sitting-room and business in Kensington. If he were to buy a property, it would be not only to provide a home for Helena but also to put up a dozen or more young people for training weekends. He began to inspect houses for sale around Epping Forest.

In June 1965 he was driving through a remote Essex village when he spotted a bungalow. "This could be it," he exclaimed as he prowled round looking through every window. "It's ideal for me, and we could have at least fifty camping on that lawn." Nor did he doubt that God would supply the money. "Lord, send me £1,000 from the sale of my book," he prayed. The next day at his publishers he asked those present to join him in a prayer of thanksgiving for the success of his book. An American voice interjected a few 'Amens', and he discovered that it belonged to Mr. Pat Zondervan, head of a large publishing firm. "I've read your book," remarked Zondervan, "and I would like to publish it in America." Whereupon he ordered a thousand copies. This was God's answer to George's prayer of faith for £1,000 and in hot excitement he phoned the estate agent. He was chagrined to hear that it had just been sold. "Why, Lord? Why?" he lamented. "Never before have I wanted anything so much as that bungalow. This must be one of your 'No's."

Apart from his personal need of a home outside the Centre, George considered the Mayflower should also acquire a country property of its own. None of the weekend camping sites were ideal and he had clashed with the wardens of each in turn. Since it was inconceivable that the Mayflower would undertake to run a country house without his supervision, he prospected with a view to fusing the two needs. As he shared his hopes with two residents he was stirred to pray with them for £10,000, and even asked a friend to start looking for a place. Two days later Hilary was informed that an old lady had left £13,000 to the Centre in her will. Another gift of hundreds of pounds' worth of timber was a further 'seal' upon God's approval. George then searched assiduously, but somehow the right property was never found.

Meanwhile George gave priority to rearing more leaders from the Sunday Group. He erected a huge board bearing the names of everyone who was helping in the clubs and groups, but he was sad to see how many had dropped away. A trio he particularly wanted to retrieve were the 'Rockers' Danny, Dave and Mo who had helped with a group that went fishing. One Sunday afternoon, as he lay unwell, he kept thinking of these boys and called his current aide, Robin Ewbank, to pray about them. "Take the Sunday Group to see Mo in hospital," he instructed. "He'd love to see them all." Then he started reading the Bible which he had neglected for several days and became wrapped in prayer. Danny, Dave, Mo, John and Janet thronged into his mind. Back in bed he could not rest and obeyed the call to get up. He strolled into the dining-room and sitting there were Danny, Dave, and three others. He was annoyed, for they were not allowed to be there at that time. Then he realised that God had arranged this situation for him to talk to these very boys. "Come upstairs and we'll have a bit of a party," he invited them each in turn. "I'll order some eggy bacon and cakes." The others refused but Danny and Dave spent the next two hours with him. He showed them the gaps on his lists of names and they eagerly volunteered to help on two club nights. As the boys went, George met John and Janet and, instead of attending the service, talked to them about their group.

Later that evening he dealt with another group and nerved a young couple to win souls. "The key thing," he advised, "is being willing to do whatever God wants you to do." As he turned wearily to bed George thanked God for the past ten hours of ceaseless counselling.

Many of the ambitious schemes which George devised remained pipe dreams. He envisaged a club room set aside for visual aids about the Bible where models of the Temple, maps of the Holy Land and life-sized pictures illustrating Bible stories could be displayed. But he lacked the time to see it through.

Realising that the youngsters made heavy weather of the Bible, he cherished the hope of translating it himself into Canning Town English. He drafted a free paraphrase of the events leading up to the death of Christ, and passed round copies to several teenagers. Then on reflection he decided to leave the task to others.

The triumph of his book, however, spurred him to write another one and he asked David Hewitt, "Will you write down all you can about prayer and especially all the wonderful answers we have had?" David obligingly compiled a hundred pages of notes as the foundation of the next book.

The summer of 1965 saw George returning to Palestine with David for another long leave. His main object was to film the sacred sites and for that he had bought a new automatic ciné camera. He rehearsed the shots and even the commentary which he could give to the Mayflower family, but to his mortification the camera failed him and his films were ruined.

The highlight of the holiday was his stay in Malta as guest of Admiral Sir John Hamilton, Commander-in-Chief of the Mediterranean Fleet. George had been invited to advise about club work among the sailors and this was the highest rung of his social climb. He exulted in his hour of glory.

CHAPTER 13

The Last Enemy

"Hilary, there's going to be a dreadful disaster." It was October 1965, and George had disturbed the secretary to inquire if the Sheppards were back from a weekend in Oxford. He was always uneasy while they were away, but now he suddenly stiffened as he confided his foreboding.

Two weeks later the troubles started. Grace Sheppard was admitted to hospital with suspected appendicitis, and the next day Skipper called the staff to share with them the shocking news that Grace had had a major operation for a malignant growth. George broke the stunned silence. "Thank God I parted on good terms with Grace. We have never been closer than in the last few weeks." He visited her in hospital and talked with her about her attitude to cancer. While Skipper accompanied Grace on her convalescence, George shouldered added burdens. "I won't say things are easy," he wrote; "in fact, Satan has been more at work in the last few weeks than at any other time."

His own wheezing and coughing persisted, but although he had been told he was suffering from bronchial asthma, extensive tests revealed nothing. He tried to accept this verdict and continued to keep a finger in every pie. He pursued personal work among his Senior Leaders and adult church members, visiting them in their homes. He organised prayer meetings, arranged jobs for club members, planned the next summer holiday for a large party of church families, wrote letters on behalf of boys in trouble, and made phone calls about equipment, building repairs and others' personal problems. The Teenage club alone seemed to suffer from the rarity of his appearances.

With a high temperature he forced himself to speak at a conference at the New Year of 1966. After his initial session he carried on for a further four hours, talking, advising and witnessing. He ran temperatures of over 100 every night for some weeks after that, and yet he led the Sunday Group on two weekends away. The second was almost too much for him. He quarrelled violently with the proprietors and retired to bed, only to emerge yelling at the teenagers for disturbing him. This was not the Mr. Burton they knew.

For some months Jean had contemplated leaving the Centre. Her enforced position as George's chaperon created strains for both of them and in a moment of vicious candour he had exploded, "Get out, I don't need you any more." Further exchange was pointless, so without saying a word even to Skipper, one February midnight Jean quitted, this time for good.

George reacted in sullen rage. Deep down he realised it was inevitable, but after eight years he dreaded the partnership being split, and shrank from people blaming him for it. He made a show of resigning, but Jean was certain that her task had been done and held firm against threats and pleas alike.

Within two days the news spread like wildfire that George was in hospital. "That's the best news I've heard for a long time," commented one church member, hoping that he would at last be forced to rest. He was especially cheered by a well-timed letter from a former Sunday Group member then in New Zealand announcing his conversion.

Word of his resignation was met with dismay and unbelief. "You can retire or die Mr. Burton, but not resign." A troubled conscience pricked one of his 'Rockers' into admitting, "I know we played you up a lot, but even so it wouldn't be the same without good old Mr. Burton." Another boy wrote, "When you was away last summer it was as if the Mayflower had half her crew missing."

Nurses protested helplessly at the string of visitors. To one who came a second time George said, "Don't come so often. Get in the queue." Ted Levitt brought him some fruit. "I don't want *that*: I want to see you, not your fruit." Helena was at his bedside daily. Investigations revealed a rapidly growing cancer and his left lung had to be removed. Skipper once more persuaded him to withdraw his hasty resignation and George determined to fight his way back to the Mayflower and till then to handle things even from hospital.

His closest assistants, especially now Joan de Torre, were constantly summoned to his bedside to take notes and letters. He kept a list of everyone who had cared enough to write to him, acknowledging them all in a duplicated letter. After his operation he asked Skipper why he could not pray. "Because you're down physically," Skipper replied. "It's our job to do the praying now. You lie back and get better."

His mood during canvalescence was one of strange acquiescence. He tried to forget his own pain as he conversed with other patients and entered into a discussion group led by the medical social worker. A card to Eva brought her and her family to him the very next day. Jean came too and they strolled in the garden, his first walk outside for two months. He wrote telling her of the letters he had received from his three sisters. He was noticing the unfolding buds of a magnolia tree. "It is fantastic that now I know the different names of birds."

Back in London a course of radiotherapy left him depressed. Helena's tempting meals and Joan's constant reassurance built up his strength, but his apparent optimism thinly masked his fear. One day as Hilary was driving him to the hospital a hearse swung in front of them. They watched it silently for a while, and then he pronounced, "I'll be the next one in the black box."

In Brian Hessian's book, *Determined to Live* he read, "You have got to believe in the power of the human body to get well: but also you have got to have an utter determination to live." George had that determination, for he was terrified of death and had faced the prospect as soon as he was rushed to hospital. When he learnt that the ward sister was a Christian, he confided his feelings to her, thinking that she would understand. "This is no way for a Christian to talk," came her rebuke, and it plunged him into deeper despondency. When Skipper tried to help him face the fact of death he flew into such a temper that he refused to speak to him for days.

George was distressed by the common question, "Why has God allowed this to happen to me?" Skipper lent him H. L. Ellison's book on Job and there he read, "Nothing exists without God's will and permission. Satan is God's creation, his power is derived from God, and willingly or unwillingly he is working out God's purpose." Satan was displaying his permitted power, but God was still in control, and a friend reminded him, "The devil only attacks hard when there is a great blessing to follow."

But throughout the month of June the devil did seem to grip George's life. News that his friend David Hewitt was asking Jean to marry him stabbed like an act of treachery. He had never quite swallowed the fact of Jean's walk-out, and as for David, he was counting on his help with the next book. Now he felt he had irrevocably lost them both and hit back with an abusive letter. Hilary discreetly removed his supply of sleeping tablets. Isolated and shut up in his room, bereft of his closest friends, refusing to speak to the Sheppards and apparently cut off from God Himself, the sick man screamed out to be loved. The few he regarded as still loyal attended him constantly, executing with trained obedience his orders for trays of food and cups of tea.

George's mood was so thunderous that Skipper asked himself, as he had in the early days of their partnership, if this was 'demon possession'. "Lord, if he is like that when I see him next," he prayed, "I will command the demon to come out of him." But before then Grace had effected a reconciliation by coming to George's aid when he was seized with a grisly coughing fit. "Grace, come and give us a kiss," George appealed. Skipper found him still in low spirits, but calm. God seemed to be saying, "This is not demon possession, it is part of George's make-up. Your duty is the same as it has been for eight years: to go on loving and accepting him and taking the strain."

But George still could not pray, and in bitterness at his chastening he could not speak about God to others. A working-party of schoolboys came, but he remained shut in his room unable to face them. And then a letter arrived. "I came to do a week's work at the Mayflower six years ago," George read. "What you told me about daily obedience to the Lord and the value of people proved a turning point in my spiritual life." "I'll go and see those boys," George responded and he told them about the letter. He was soon in full spate, urging them to commit themselves to the Lord Jesus Christ.

The storm cloud had passed and George could once more meet God's eyes and pray. He poured out his heart that night, telling God of his fears and anger, telling Him that he accepted whatever the future might bring. The next day his changed outlook was obvious to all. "I don't want to die. I want to live and serve God. But I'm no longer afraid to meet Him, for I know that He will accept me. I can't *feel* peace, but I know that I *have* peace with God through the blood of Jesus Christ."

What was the nature of this peace which Jesus had bequeathed to his disciples? Was it peace of mind? If so, it had eluded George all his life. He had grappled with the problem some months earlier.

"It is easy to say that the Christian has this peace all the time in Christ. In theory this may be true, but in practice it is not. When we cannot understand the reason for our suffering we are rebellious and lose our peace of mind. God often takes away our peace of mind to teach us more about Himself. We should not seek for peace by itself instead of seeking for Christ and serving Him."

These words were to form part of his second book, and the goal of completing it reinforced his will to recover. He would pull the material into shape during his August holiday in Switzerland. David was now cut out of his life, so George had to rely on other friends: Joan, Rosemary, Matthew and Christopher. Helena was only prevented from coming by the final illness of her sister Mariska. George and Chris would fly to Geneva where the others would meet them with the dormobile. "We'll tour and stop at camp sites," he directed, "and have some time round the Bible, but not lots of holy huddles." The holiday was designed to fortify him for the Mayflower family holiday in Blankenburge which was to follow it. Any doubts about the wisdom of such a rest-cure were quelled by a check-up at the hospital. "Yes, you go," the doctor confirmed. "It will do you good."

At the Council meeting held before his departure, George asked Skipper to hold a Communion service. He wept unashamedly as he shook the hands of those he used to resent but had come to respect.

George and his friends spent a week camping on a slope overlooking Lake Geneva. He reviewed past struggles with staff and residents and looked forward with some apprehension to the day when his Senior Leaders would enter into full partnership with the staff. Together they read St. Paul's great chapter on love (I Corinthians, chapter thirteen), the chapter that used to 'rip him to pieces'. "You've all shown me love," he acknowledged. "I could never have taken what you have taken from me. I thank God for each one of you."

Those quiet days were followed by nightmare strains. They moved to another camp site at Zurich where a rainstorm forced them to retire to a guest house. But George was now racked by pneumonia and on Sunday, August 7th had to be admitted to hospital. The doctor's visit and injection brought a moment of terror, but prayer calmed him. "Tell my wife I am ill," he requested Joan. "Tell Skipper there's no man like him; and Grace too. I love them both. Jean and David—I want them to know that I ask their forgiveness and anyone else I have wronged." Then closing his eyes he murmured triumphantly, "I have peace through the blood of Jesus Christ. It's wonderful. Now I *know* what the peace of God means." In a phone call to Skipper the next day he reported that now at last he was experiencing peace.

On Tuesday morning the four friends gathered at the hospital. True to form he bade Rosemary take a photograph of him, but she had not brought her camera and this evoked a burst of wrath. They sang, 'How good is the God we adore'. Even George joined in, and was still sufficiently in command to interrupt them with orders to sing more quietly. "You'll wake up the man in the next bed," he scolded. "Now you must go and I'll see you all at five o'clock." They left him for the last time with an expression of complete peace on his face, in strange contrast with the turbulence of the past.

CHAPTER 14

The Legacy

"I won' 'arf miss 'im 'ollerin' an' shoutin' at me," said a stout woman wistfully, watching the coffin being carried away from the Mayflower chapel. The defiantly red coach, laden with silent teenagers, caught the eye in the long procession to the cemetery. A string of scooters followed. As the first Senior Leaders joined Helena and other relatives round the open grave, David Sheppard led the crowd in singing, triumphantly, 'Jesus Christ is Risen Today'.

"George was a very earthy man," Skipper had just been saying. "What a lesson for us that God could take someone with such weaknesses, fears and problems and use him to bless other people so mightily. God has placed His treasure of the gospel in earthenware pots like this, so that people would not say, 'What a wonderful pot!' but, 'What a wonderful treasure!' "

The crowd dispersed and Helena lingered to look at the wreaths. Among them lay one from gangster Bobby who had been the ringleader of a club George had run for a time in his early days at the Mayflower. When he went to prison not long after closing the club George visited him, and later attended his wedding.

A pale, slim orphan girl stood weeping. "He was like a father to me, and now I've no one," she sobbed. A couple moved up beside her representing a score of others who had been inspired by George's example to open their home to groups of teenagers.

The mourners pooled memories of their friend. "He'd still be with us if he had rested more," said one. "I bet they know all about the Mayflower up There." "Now that Mr. Burton's gone I suppose there'll be no Sunday Group," a former resident observed to Jim Gosling. "You're wrong," Jim replied, "because Mr. Burton often used to say, 'If you ever build a set-up round yourself, it'll collapse when you've gone'. He has been preparing for this."

"Your work at the Mayflower will endure," Jack Wallace had

written to George some months earlier, in response to his umpteenth and final resignation, "for it consists of living people whom you have sought to present mature in Christ Jesus. Your warmth as a man and honesty as a Christian have won you a place in the hearts of many outside Canning Town, of whom I am certainly one. I am —and will, I hope, continue to be—known as a friend of George Burton."

Ted Lyons was one whom George had patiently nurtured and developed. It seemed as if history was repeating itself when Ted spoke on the B.B.C.'s 'People's Service' about a group of twelve boys which he had been running for the past few years.

"One boy was the leader of the group and I would work through Micky. I always believed that he would be a Christian leader, but first I had to get him to accept Christ. He used to hear me and others speak about Christian stuff, and after about three years he became a Christian. It was just the first step, but Christ did go into his life.

"For a time he went on O.K. as a Christian. I remember once he had a fight in the club, and so the other boy kept away. I was worried and used to say to Micky, 'Well, do you think you could go round and see him?' I thought, if he can get the boy to come back, and not me, this would be terrific. Well, he did go round and Dave did come back, and I could see in that the real power of Christ.

"After some time he got into the company of some lads who had been in trouble. They did a bit of stealing and were caught and Micky was sent to the Scrubs. For me this was a disaster—a boy who I had spent a lot of time with had ended up in prison. But I do believe that God is still in Micky and when Micky comes out God will still accept him, because I know that God has accepted me back after the things I got up to."

Not many years before, George could have been speaking in almost identical language about Ted himself. The hope, which he had often expressed to the young people, that they would learn to pass on to others the same love and understanding which they had received, was beginning to be realised.

Some months after George's death David Sheppard was in the chapel commissioning fifteen men and women who had been elected by the whole church; alongside them stood representatives of the staff and Council. "Will you as members of the Mayflower Committee serve God and His Church, and seek His will in the affairs of the Mayflower Family Centre?"

"I will do so, the Lord being my helper," they chorused. There was Jim, a married man in his twenties now and a tried leader, many of his mannerisms, as well as his concern for others, displaying George Burton's abiding influence. With him were two more of the Senior Leaders, Rita and Ted. The adult members included Rich, Fred, Jim Waller, both of Ted's parents and others whom George had helped and visited, sought and won, taught and loved. Another was Bob Halsey, now resident in 'The Buildings', the block of flats which had so attracted George when he first came to Canning Town. Actively involved in plans for developing a community centre, Bob was realising George's early prayers for Christian homes to be established in those flats.

George, more than anyone else, had laboured for this day. "We are going to have a Church Committee," he predicted three years earlier. "But we will wait until we have a lot of adults who know Christ, and can reason together as a Christian team." But God knew that George Burton could never have submitted to being bound by their decisions; and so this step of partnership between the Council, the staff and the local church could now be taken.

Here stood the representatives of the Mayflower church, people who mattered to George Burton, his epitaph. In their lives and the impact of their homes lay the key to the spread of the gospel of Jesus Christ through Canning Town and beyond.